CRISIS
PREACHING

CRISIS PREACHING

Personal and Public

JOSEPH R. JETER JR.

ABINGDON
Nashville

Crisis Preaching

Copyright © 1998 by Joseph R. Jeter Jr.

This book is printed on recycled, acid-free paper.

Jeter, Joseph R.
  Crisis preaching : personal and public / Joseph R. Jeter, Jr.
    p.   cm.
  Includes bibliographical references.
  ISBN 0-687-07392-8 (pbk. : alk. paper)
  1. Preaching.   I. Title.
BV4211.2.J47   1998
251'.56—dc21   98-19372
                                                          CIP

Unless otherwise noted, Scripture quotations are from the New Revised Standard Version Bible. Copyright © 1989 by the Division of Christian Education of the National Council of the Churches of Christ in the USA. Used by permission.

Scripture quotations noted KJV are from the King James Version Bible.

Andraé Crouch, "Through It All," Copyright 1971 by Manna Music, Inc., 35255 Brooten Road, Pacific City, OR 97135. All Rights Reserved. Used with permission.

"The Prayer of the Old Horse," from PRAYERS FROM THE ARK by Carmen Bernos de Gasztold, translated by Rumer Godden, Translation copyright © 1962, renewed 1990 by Rumer Godden. Original copyright 1947, © 1955 by Editions du Cloitre. Used by permission of Viking Penguin, a division of Penguin Putnam Inc.

Diagram on p. 101 is reproduced from STRAIGHT TALK ABOUT TEACHING IN TODAY'S CHURCH by Locke E. Bowman, Jr. © MCMLXVII The Westminster Press. Used by permission of Westminster John Knox Press.

98 99 00 01 02 03 04 05 06 07 — 10 9 8 7 6 5 4 3 2 1

MANUFACTURED IN THE UNITED STATES OF AMERICA

For
the Reverend Dr. Robert John Sargent

CONTENTS

INTRODUCTION

Y ou wake up on a Sunday morning feeling good! Your sermon—finished on Thursday, of course—lies safely nestled in your desk. You know it is no great shakes as a sermon—a little excursus on "love" or perhaps some warmed over Reinhold Niebuhr—but it will do, and you are looking forward to a good morning. You pad out in your slippers to get the paper, stop, glance at the headlines, and watch your nice little sermon turn to ashes before your eyes. The headlines scream of crisis and in less than four hours your people will gather, anxious to hear the Word of God for the day. It has happened to me. It has happened, or will happen, to you.

In November 1963, Gene Boutellier was the pastor of the Christian Church in Fresno, California. Late one Friday morning came the shocking news that the President had been assassinated. Not knowing what to do, Boutellier stumbled up the steps into the church tower, grabbed the rope, and began ringing the bell. He rang the bell until he could pull the rope no longer. Then he came down the steps, chest heaving, and walked through the door into the chancel. To his utter astonishment, he found the sanctuary packed, every pew filled, every eye on him. When I first heard this story, I leaned forward and asked, "What did he say?" But, alas, what he said, if anything, has not entered into history.[1]

Most books on preaching address the week-by-week process of sermon preparation, as well they should. Young preachers are encouraged to plan ahead, to allow time for sermons to marinate and simmer. This is good advice. Nevertheless, my experience suggests that a number of sermons each year are preached in crisis and, given the state of our society, that number is growing. As one observer noted, "Modern existence seems to be a crisis waiting to happen.[2] Ironically, these sermons, which are among the very most important that we preach, are also those for which we have the least amount of experience, skill, and preparation time. The general "rules" on the preparation and delivery of sermons simply do not avail. As the opening stories attest, sometimes crisis sermons must be prepared in a matter of two or three hours, and sometimes they must even be conceived, composed, and delivered extemporaneously. There is no time for careful exegesis and leisurely preparation. The creative brooding in which so many sermons are conceived and gestated is cut short with a sermon that must be, as was Macduff, "from [its] mother's womb untimely ripped."

Many have been the times when I have heard preachers, overwhelmed by the task of crisis preaching, stick their heads into the sand and totally ignore the crisis, leaving listeners lost, confused, and not a little angry: "If the preacher hasn't got anything to say, what's the use . . . ?" The clumps of distressed people gathered in the parking lot after church, trying to do for each other what the preacher has been unable to do for them, is testimony to this failure of the preacher's office. On other occasions, I have heard preachers try to make light of crises, offering flippant jokes like "You think it's bad here . . . ," producing nervous titters and subvocal frustration in the congregation. Perhaps worst of all, I have heard preachers couch almost every crisis in terms of divine punishment.

It is clear that investigation of this matter is needed. In this book I propose to enumerate some of the crises that have an impact on our pulpit ministries; reflect on those crises psychologically, theologically, and homiletically; suggest methods and resources for crisis preaching; and offer some crisis sermons as models. Throughout the book I have tried to be conscious of the need not only for clear concepts but also for vivid imagery, so that preachers and their people might not only hear but also see approaches to crisis preaching that work.

My hope is that this book will be useful to preachers both in and out of crisis. What has been said of the weather applies to ministry: if your ministry is crisis-free at the moment, stick around! While all of us tend to put off fixing the roof because it is not raining now, we know better. The same is true of preaching in crisis. As James Oglesby has said, "When crisis comes . . . if you don't have a faith, you don't have time to go out and get one; if you don't have a relationship with your people, it's too late to build one."[3] Similarly, if we do not know how to preach in crisis situations, it is difficult to learn in the middle of one. I once gave some lectures on crisis preaching to a group of ministers at Bethany College in West Virginia and received a polite response. One morning during the conference several of us who have difficulty beginning our day without a newspaper were waiting for the arrival of the paper from Pittsburgh. When it came, the banner headline read: "Wheeling-Pittsburgh Steel Declares Bankruptcy." The ministers, many of whom would be going back that afternoon to congregations that overnight had become fifty percent unemployed, came over and said, "Joey, could we go over this stuff again." I did a repeat, crash course for them, but it would have been better if they and their congregations had already done the kind of work that would have prepared them for preaching and living more effectively through that crisis. My hope is that this book may aid in that process for the next time the world tumbles in. For it will.

I am grateful to Brite Divinity School for the summer stipend that allowed me to complete this work; to Jeff

Powers, Stephanie Cobb, and Rick Hamilton for their help; and to my wife, Brenda, and son, Justin, for their love and encouragement. The work is dedicated to my father-in-law, the Reverend Dr. Robert John Sargent, who has been a mentor to me in both preaching and plumbing, two of life's greatest mysteries.

CHAPTER ONE

TYPES OF CRISES

What is a crisis? R. L. Pavelsky defines crisis as "an upset in homeostasis,"[1] a clinical way of assessing that loss of balance which W. B. Yeats described more poetically: "Things fall apart; the centre cannot hold."[2] More formally, Charles Gerkin describes a crisis as an extreme or boundary condition in which "the fundamental contradiction between human aspirations and finite possibilities becomes visible in such a way as to demand attention."[3] Harry Emerson Fosdick defined it in more passionate language:

> "Deep trouble," we say, not broad, long, high—those adjectives would not apply—but "deep trouble." When the psalmist says, "Out of the depths have I cried unto thee, O Lord," we know what he means. He is in trouble.[4]

However we choose to describe it, Yeats's observation holds, things do fall apart in a crisis, including centered selves. How are we to grasp the substance of these events, the manner of disintegration, and ways to endure or perhaps even prevail? On the one hand, there are as many *types* of crises as there are *crises*, because events are unique. Nevertheless, crisis events may be grouped and described by certain characteristics they have in common.

From a preacher's perspective, there are three types of crises that tend to interrupt our orderly homiletical agenda:

public, congregational, and personal. Of those I call public, there are political crises: war, assassination, riot and other great civic upheavals. It would be very interesting in this regard to have a sampling of sermons preached across the United States at evening worship on Sunday, December 7, 1941. We do, however, have collections of sermons preached following the assassination of President Kennedy in 1963, the Los Angeles riots in 1992, and the bombing of the federal building in Oklahoma City on April 19, 1995.[5]

There are also other disasters, natural or otherwise: storm, flood, fire, famine, terrible accidents, and so forth. My friend Randy Updegraff Spleth was pastor of the Hillside Christian Church in San Bernardino, California, in 1981, when the infamous Panorama fire raged through town on a Friday morning. The church was almost the only building left standing in a square mile area. After thirty-six hours of continuous relief work, Randy had to climb into the pulpit on Sunday to face an overflow of stunned and homeless people. How many times recently have we read of fires and gas plant explosions and tornadoes roaring through towns and churches and wondered, "What did the preachers say?"

This type of crisis spills over into what may be called congregational crises, those that affect or infect or afflict the particular congregations we serve. The pastor in San Antonio whose youth group and leaders were killed in a ski-trip bus accident: what did he preach about the next Sunday? All who have been in the parish for any length of time have probably experienced the trauma of having some pillar of the church fall dead in the middle of worship. What do you do? What do you say? In the congregation there are also financial crises, scandals, crises of dissension and direction, all crying for a word of wisdom and grace.

Finally, there are personal crises, those that strike the preacher directly and personally. These include personal tragedy, illness, being fired, loss of faith, and others. So many times we step into the pulpit out of the wreckage of our own lives. What do we say? Such times have been the occasion for some of the best and worst sermons ever preached. When Arthur John Gossip's wife suddenly died, he walked through his pain into the pulpit and preached a sermon entitled "But When Life Tumbles In, What Then?" It may be, put quite simply, the greatest sermon ever preached in the English language.[6] Then there was the preacher in the Texas Panhandle some years back who dealt with a crisis by preaching against his enemies in the congregation and finished his sermon by pulling a revolver from under the pulpit and shooting the chairman of the elders.

Of course, there are some preachers for whom every sermon is a personal crisis, because they never begin work on their sermons until Saturday night or Sunday morning. That is a hazard not covered by the policy of this book and I have no succor to offer, except to observe that this practice will eventually bring their preaching ministries down—which will precipitate, of course, another crisis!

One might imagine a rather large body of literature from which to draw on this topic. But I know of no other book which seeks to do what this one does. Ronald J. Allen's *Preaching the Topical Sermon* addresses crisis sermons among others. David Buttrick's chapters on preaching and praxis (24 and 25) in his *Homiletic* are concerned with "addressing persons in lived experience,"[7] and some of that "lived experience" occurs in the context of crisis. Kelly Miller Smith's 1983 Beecher Lectures at Yale, published under the title *Social Crisis Preaching,* confront one aspect of crisis preaching. Beyond those, there are a few articles, some collections of crisis sermons, and little else. A bibliography will be found at the end of this book.

CHAPTER TWO

PSYCHOLOGY OF THE CRISIS EXPERIENCE

t has been more than half a century since Harry Emerson Fosdick uttered his famous dictum that preaching is "counseling on a group scale." Given the broad appeal of that statement, one might expect that it had considerable impact on the disciplines of preaching and pastoral counseling, that it led to joint efforts between homileticians and pastoral theologians, that it produced cross-fertilized literature. Such has not been the case. Experts in counseling have had little to say about that form of "group counseling" called preaching.[1] Howard Clinebell has written:

> Growthful preaching offers a regular opportunity to communicate the Christian message...in a life-affirming, esteem-strengthening, growth-nurturing, and challenging way....By being involved, through pastoral care in the problems and hopes, fears and dreams of their people, preachers can bring the wisdom of the Bible to bear on the real concerns of people.... Preaching often leads to pastoral counseling opportunities.[2]

And that is about it. Nor have homileticians made significant contributions to the counseling dimensions of preaching. While some pastoral theologians have pointed out similarities and a possible relationship between counseling and preaching, few have taken the question beyond those initial observations. Man of many hats William Willimon flatly denies that preaching can be "counseling on a group scale," in which the preacher becomes a "stand-up shrink." The two functions of ministry may be mutually supportive and enriching, he says, but "they must be kept distinct."[3] Interestingly though, just as preaching is moving away from a two-decades-long preoccupation with form, pastoral care is also returning from its even longer tryst with secular psychotherapy.[4] Howard Stone's *The Word of God and Pastoral Care* deals explicitly with a theology of proclamation. However, all of Stone's resources are persons in his own discipline, theologians and biblical scholars. No homileticians are to be found.

The fear of stepping outside one's field of knowledge is intimidating. And I feel it now. This section does not seek converts for Fosdick's dictum, but it does assume that persons preach more effectively when they better understand the human condition. What do people experience in crisis situations? How do they respond? What help do they need from preachers? Can we speak to that need? What are they able to hear or not hear? These are important questions, but ones which most homileticians have avoided. So I turn to the work of pastoral theologians, psychologists, and counselors to reflect upon their work homiletically. In future works, I hope the encounter may be less reactive and more proactive.

There is significant literature on what counselors call crisis intervention. Important resources include chapter 8 of Howard Clinebell's revised *Basic Types of Pastoral Care and Counseling,* Howard Stone's *Crisis Counseling,* and David Switzer's *Minister as Crisis Counselor.* Stone suggests that the two basic types of crises are developmental and situational.[5] Developmental crises are those expected as persons move through their lives, and include such crises as learning to walk, puberty, marriage, and so forth.[6] That they are expected makes them no less painful. If such transitional crises are not handled well, they can have long-term effects. Situational or accidental crises are "exceptional and unpredictable upheavals resulting from unusual circumstances."[7]

Andrew Lester further subdivides situational crises into two categories: *interruptive* and *eruptive*.[8] Interruptive crises have an *external* origin. They come upon people unbidden and unexpected. They can be public, congregational, or personal. Interruptive crises, like a hurricane, are very traumatic and have long-term consequences. A year after the devastation wrought by Hurricane Andrew in Florida in 1992, Carl Dudley and Melvin Schoonover wrote:

> [The local pastors] all agreed that surviving the storm was easy compared with survival afterward. Pastors who were astonished at the low death toll at the height of the wind are now equally astonished and dismayed at the number of parishioners and neighbors who are dying as a consequence of the storm. "Stress-related deaths continue to haunt our congregation long after the storm," said one distraught pastor. "Like the debris in our community, some people simply cannot get their lives together in this constant uncertainty." The spiritual impact of losing control still extracts life and energy from those who survived.[9]

Unlike interruptive crises, which come from without, eruptive crises *break out from within*. While persons tend to know the cause of the interruptive crisis, they sometimes do not know the reason for the eruptive crisis. They may not understand why they feel the way they do. It may be unresolved grief, shame, or guilt about acts and deeds done or undone, or something altogether unknown. It has been said that more than ten percent of a congregation is depressed on any given Sunday. It is also important for preachers to realize that, although they are generally informed about interruptive crises, they may never know about many eruptive ones. For example, preachers may know about the interruptive crisis surrounding the birth of a mentally disabled child. But they may never know about the eruptive guilt over the mother's drug use during the pregnancy.

Lester also reminds us that in crisis situations our future stories, including our visions of God's future and our part in it, take a big and painful hit.[10] So we are not dealing simply with what has happened to us in the past, or the mess we are in now, but how these things affect, and sometimes shred, our hopes and plans for the future. The current epidemic of gang activity among young people testifies to the truth of this assessment. So many people are at a loss to understand why young people join gangs and engage in criminal activity. Do these young people not realize that if they continue on this path, they will, probably within two to three years, end up in prison or dead? Yes, they realize it. But it simply does not concern many of them, because if you have no positive future story, no hope of building an interesting, rewarding life for yourself, then what happens in the future does not matter to you.

Summarizing, crises are developmental or situational in nature. Situational crises may be interruptive (external) or eruptive (internal). These crises may be seen as permanent or temporary. While preachers occasionally deal with developmental crises, such as leaving home, marriage, parenthood, midlife crisis, retirement, and death (though rarely with others such as toilet-training, oedipal conflict, and menopause), we are more and more frequently forced to confront (or avoid) situational crises. The focus of this book is upon situational crises, primarily interruptive, but also eruptive, and the lack of hope for the future that may be present among the people to whom we preach.

There is yet another factor at work here. While a sermon may have been occasioned by a crisis in the life of one person, we generally preach on such crises only when they have become community crises. I may indeed counsel with John about his use of steroids to enhance athletic performance, but I do not preach about it. However, when John goes into a "'roid rage," grabs a gun and murders his family, the whole community of faith is thrown into crisis. And homiletical engagement is demanded.

What happens to people in crisis? Life is full of problems, but not all problems evolve into crises. Generally, people are thrown into crisis when their usual methods of dealing with problems and any additional trial-and-error methods they may come up with to reduce the rising anxiety all prove ineffective.[11] Crises tend to produce several kinds of responses in people that can be addressed homiletically: anger, confusion, grief, fear, and guilt are among them. More than one of these responses may be operative in any one crisis. And since we are preaching to a group, this is more likely than not. Further, the logically or abstractly stated concern may differ from and be overwhelmed by the intrapsychic one. Consider a preacher in Sarajevo during the war-torn summer of 1995. Which concern was more basic for his or her people at that point in their lives: the biblical concern for peace or paralyzing fear? A preacher who extols the joy of the resurrection promise to a congregation which has seen a busload of its finest youth swept away in a flood may ignore the volcanic grief that underlies the moment. People do not come to church to hear their preacher offer her or his plan for achieving a diplomatic resolution to the crisis in Bosnia. They come because they believe, or they hope, that there is a Word from God for their anger, confusion, grief, fear, and guilt. And this, of course, makes crisis a theological concern.

CHAPTER THREE

THEOLOGY AND CRISIS

The primary problem facing preaching today is theological.[1] What does the church have to say that is worth hearing? Or pressing further, what is God saying to the world today that we need to hear? A professor once told a student that he had preached a wonderful sermon, except for what he said and how he said it. Most homiletical attention for the past two decades has been focused on how we say things. However, I believe the malaise infecting mainstream Protestantism is at base a lack of anything important to say. So we are called back to the theological task. And it is not easy. In the same way that pastoral theologians have warned about the separation of theology from pastoral care, homileticians point out the uncomfortable relationship that exists between theology and preaching. Both point to problems that emerge when systematic theology is transferred unmodified to the sermon or another caregiving situation.[2] A counseling session or a sermon is not simply a vehicle for systematic theology. Rather, these are events which require effective pastoral theology and homiletical theology. Paul Scott Wilson says, "The sermon is not the dilution of theology; it is rather the completion of theology, made complete through Christ speaking it and constituting the church through it."[3] And as we strive to do our theology hard against the twenty-first century, we find to our discomfort that the "rules" have changed. As Susan White puts it:

Can we now confess and intercede before a God who seems not to have heard the cries of the Jews in the death camps? Do we want absolution from a God whom we have found guilty of indifference? Can we use the psalms which speak of the decisive intervention of God in situations of distress and injustice? Can we declare in the Lord's Supper that this is a God who has the power to save? Can we, in short, pray in the same way to the God of classical theism, the God of power, wisdom, might, and mercy, as a post-Auschwitz community of faith.[4]

White speaks of doing theology after a crisis (post-Auschwitz), making this a good place to point out the critical importance of theological engagement before and after crisis situations. As we have already heard, "If you don't have a faith when a crisis comes, you don't have time to go out and get one." Preaching is a siege, not a blitzkrieg.[5] Part of the homiletical task is the slow painstaking development of faith that will stand when the storms come.

Some years ago there was a church that had two busloads of young people at camp swept away in a flash flood with a high loss of life. I went to hear one of the pastors preach the next day. I came away impressed with his faith and his compassion. Years later, though he no longer served that church, I managed to find him and invite him to speak with students about his experience. He graciously consented. Of the sermon he preached, he remembered nothing. He said, "I was pleaded out. I could not think. I could not cry. Whatever I said was just a gift of the Holy Spirit." And I believe grace works like that, tempering the wind to the shorn lamb.

During this visit he went on to speak of the two things that saw the church through the tragedy: submission to the will of God and the sense of family that existed in the church. "It was a severe mercy," he said, "but we yielded ourselves to God's will. And we were a family. We all cared about one another." He told us that the church was reenergized and began to grow. It grew for the next eighteen months or so, and they even completed a building project. Sounds good.

But then in various ways he began to talk about what happened after that. He did not put all these things together, and frankly, I am not sure he was aware of the implications of what he said to us. After about eighteen months, the church stopped growing. How many of the families that lost young people were still in the church? None. How many of the young people that survived the tragedy were still in the church? None. How many of the ministers and staff at the time were still serving the congregation? None. And, he confessed, years later he still woke in the night screaming and drenched with sweat. He was still haunted.

There are no doubt other ways to understand this, but the only explanation that I can give for what happened to him and his congregation is that a too shallow understanding of the will of God and a too facile claim about church as family were an insufficient theological foundation upon which to stand. It looked good for about eighteen months and then it washed away. He did the right thing, I believe, on the Sunday following the tragedy: "Dear God, it hurts so bad. It is so hard to walk this road. Please walk it with us." But the slow, patient construction of a faith big enough to stand against such a terrible disaster did not occur, either before or after the event. It has been said, correctly I believe, that the second year after a tragedy is often worse than the first.

Part of the minister's task is therefore to preach in preparation for crisis. Some time back my teacher Ronald Osborn wrote to tell me about a new preacher coming to the town where he lives. The announcement in the local paper contained the news that the preacher had won an award in "pre-aching" while she was in seminary. Osborn was puzzled. Was this award for exemplary advance empathy toward people's pain? Finally, it dawned on him that it was dumb word division and not pre-suffering identification. She had won a preaching award, not a pre-aching one! I remembered that, because preaching *does* have a pre-aching (or, to get fancy, pre-tribulation) role to play. One way to fulfill this responsibility, beyond the regular, faithful proclamation of the gospel, is to ask specifically: What questions and problems are likely to confront my people during a crisis? Preach on them. Fosdick is reported to have said that, like trees in a storm, we may say that our concern is the high winds when, in fact, our concern is our rootage. Preaching preaching provides rootage.

Then, after the crisis has abated—and remembering that for some people certain crises never completely go away—these same concerns can be re-presented with the crisis itself as the landscape for the message. "Do you remember how we felt when the church burned down, what we said and what we did? Now let's talk about what God has done in our midst since that day, rebuilding us as we rebuilt the sanctuary." A sidebar here: I learned years ago as a young pastor to mark the one-year anniversary of a death in my calendar for the next year. I may have forgotten about it, but the family will not, and a pastoral contact can be important.[6]

An approach to crisis preaching must engage these theological issues at a level equal to both the concerns of the people and their ability to hear. It is not helpful in crisis to insult people's theological understanding ("God needed another angel in heaven") or to aim a message high over their perhaps diminished ability to process abstract information ("The more non-being one can subsume, the stronger one becomes"). I heard about a woman who shook hands with the preacher at the church door after he had preached during a crisis, and said to him, "Well, after listening to that sermon, at least I know your favorite biblical text." Puzzled, the preacher said, "And what might that be?" "Feed my giraffes," said the woman as she stalked out the door.[7]

CRISES OF UNDERSTANDING

So what are some of the theological concerns raised in crises? Just as crises may be divided, psychologically speaking, into developmental and situational ones, Ronald Allen suggests that, theologically speaking, they may be divided into crises of *understanding* and crises of *decision*.[8] Oversimplifying, we might say persons face crises of theology proper (understanding) and ethics (decision). In a crisis of understanding, people struggle to know what is happening and why. In a crisis of decision they struggle to know what to do in response.

We look first at crises of understanding.[9] Most of these fall into the sticky domain of theodicy. The primary theodicy question is: Is God? People often function as if *God* were one of the pins that hold up their world. When their pins are knocked out from under them, *God* is knocked away also. Most people of faith grow up understanding God to be good and powerful. When an unspeakable tragedy occurs, such reason as they can muster may lead them to conclude: "If there were a God, God would not have let this happen. Since it did happen, there cannot be a God."

One step short of this are questions about the character of God. "There may be a God, but any God who would let this happen is a monster." Crises provide the landscape for asking what God is like. Loving? Interested? Caring? Or not? Living, as we do, post-Auschwitz, we cannot escape such questions. This leads to the next theological issue. "Is God manipulable? Can we pester God into doing what we want? Should we?" In crises, God images tend to arise which are not part of our current theological understanding at all, and some of them are not very attractive.

How about Providence or God's power? "Could God have done something different in the event that precipitated this crisis? If so, why did God not do it?" This may lead to the questions, "How does God feel about me? Is God angry with me about something I have done or not done? Am I being punished?"

Questions about God's will often come up in crises. Along the line between free will and determinism, many people's understanding may be closer to the free will pole until a crisis occurs and they race toward determinism. In William Sloan Coffin's oft-quoted sermon following the death of his son, he spoke strongly against that very thing:

> Many things can be said when a person dies, but there is at least one thing that should never be said.
>
> The night after Alex died, I was sitting in the living room of my sister's house outside of Boston when the front door opened and in came a nice-looking middle-aged woman carrying about 18 quiches. When she saw me she shook her head, then headed for the kitchen, saying sadly over her shoulder, "I just don't understand the will of God."
>
> Instantly, I was up and in hot pursuit, swarming all over her. "I'll say you don't, lady!" I said. (I knew the anger would do me good, and the instruction for her was long overdue.)
>
> I continued, "Do you think it was the will of God that Alex never fixed that lousy windshield wiper of his, that he was probably driving too fast in such a storm, that he probably had had a couple of 'frosties' too many? Do you think it is God's will that there are no streetlights along that stretch of road, and no guardrail separating the road and Boston Harbor?"
>
> Nothing so infuriates me as the incapacity of seemingly intelligent people to get it through their heads that God doesn't go around this world with his fingers on triggers, his fist around knives, his hands on steering wheels. God is against all unnatural deaths. And Christ spent an inordinate amount of time delivering people from paralysis, insanity, leprosy and muteness.[10]

There is also a tremendous need to blame in many crisis situations. Why did this happen? Who is to blame? God? The devil? The self? The other? Fate? If God is to blame, what happens to the structures of our existence that depend upon God?[11] When these disintegrate, our understanding of what life means loses clarity and focus.

Rodney Hutton deals with this in an essay on blame and resolution. He suggests that we tend to perceive crises either as our fault (internal) or someone else's fault (external). Also, we may see crises as temporary and avoidable (unstable) or permanent and unavoidable (stable). This leads to four perspectives, which we often use in assessing blame in a crisis and seeking to resolve or cope with it. They are: (1) Internal-Stable: it is my fault and nothing can be done about it; (2) Internal-Unstable: I caused the crisis, but by my subsequent actions, consequences can be avoided or mitigated; (3) External-Stable: someone else has unleashed or brought about this crisis, which is now inexorable and unavoidable (close to the traditional understanding of "Fate"); and (4) External-Unstable: the crisis is not of my making, but I can do something about it.[12] Too many times we and our people tumble into assessments of crises as "stable," believing there is no way to avoid or mitigate the results and consequences. This can have a paralyzing effect on people. Or we may believe that resolution of an "unstable" crisis is totally dependent upon us and be overwhelmed by that burden.

Clinebell claims that pastoral care and counseling are ways of doing theology.[13] So is preaching. We can see the impressive presence of theological concerns attending every crisis situation in which we preach. Is God? What is God like? Why did God do or not do this to us? We must not approach the sermon as if these questions are not present among our people. And if we ignore them because they are hard questions or pretend not to see them because we would rather preach on something else, we make of the preaching ministry less than it can be.

An important word of caution comes at this point. While we should not ignore hard questions, we need, if we can, to determine which are real questions and which are, in Stone's description, *poetic questions:*

> Many of the whys clients raise are actually poetic questions. They are a symbolic or metaphoric way of expressing depths of misery. Indeed, many parishioners may find it easier to ask, "Why did God do this?" than to say, "I have had an immense loss and am feeling utterly devastated by it."[14]

Stone goes on to suggest that the pastor will seek to determine whether the people in crisis really want to engage in theological dialogue or whether they are simply seeking a way to express their pain. This is critical as one approaches the pulpit as well. The painstaking task of reconstructive theology may well come later; the more immediate task for the sermon is lamentation. This is to say that some of the questions that arise in crisis are unanswerable, in a sermon or any other way. But the pastor needs to try to discover if these are really the questions being asked.[15] In the next chapter we will consider both lamentation and ways of appropriating theological understanding and support. For now, assuming that the pastor has determined that the theological questions being asked are real and serious, let me suggest three important theological affirmations that can be made in response: *remembrance, presence,* and *promise.*

1. Remembrance

One of the dangers of a crisis is that it may cut us off from our memory. And, in one sense, the opposite of remember is not forget; the opposite of remember is dismember.[16] In this sense, then, to re/member is to be put back together, to be made right again as the people of God, an important response to the dis/membering effects of crisis. Urban T. Holmes suggests that worship is an act of memory and, more radically, that "a person with no memory is one incapable of worship."[17] When the present and future have been ripped from the past and bob without anchor on the stormy seas of crisis, what shall we do? In another connection Dietrich Ritschl suggests that:

> the Church's recognition of [the presence of Christ] enables [us] to "hope backward," i.e., that [Jesus Christ] may change and remove those elements of the past which still burden the present and destroy the hope for the future, and to "remember forward," i.e., that the promises of the past may be fulfilled in the future.[18]

The same is true of preaching in crisis. When our present and our immediate future lie in shambles, we can "hope backward," that is, we can find our hope, our anchor, in what God has done in the past, and we can then "remember" those mighty acts of God "forward" into our present and future.

The Jews who gathered around tables in the ghettos of Europe to celebrate Passover and remember why "this night is not like other nights," and the Christians who broke bread in catacombs and sang hymns in jail, did so because their memory of God's providence was the only thing between them and oblivion. Gossip put it bluntly, "You people in the sunshine may believe the faith, but we in the shadow must believe it. We have nothing else."[19]

In another context I recounted that ancient tradition about the crucifixion which says that when Jesus died and the sky turned dark, "the good women of Jerusalem lit their Sabbath lamps."[20] This tradition is generally cited to show the insensitivity of the Jews to Jesus and his mission, but I have been thinking about it. It was Friday afternoon. And there was a terrible tension in the air: a sense of Armageddon, of the shattering final clash between good and evil, a portentous, fearful time. And what would you have had the women to do? When the sky turns black in midafternoon and the stars begin to fall, shall we give up, hide in the cellar, and whimper? Or shall we light a lamp against the darkness, remember, and intone the ancient words which reaffirm our faith that, no matter what, God is with us. The more I think about what the women did, the more I respect their faith. And the more I understand that even when the Son of God dies, life goes on, or the Son of God has died in vain.

2. Presence

In the past, Christians in crisis searched for the will of God and, when the crisis resulted in tragedy and trauma, sought to yield to that will. When the son of nineteenth-century religious leader Alexander Campbell drowned in 1847, he bowed to God's will. In his words, God was "too wise to err and too kind causelessly to afflict the children of men.... We must, and do endeavor, to acquiesce in this affliction, believing that the Lord has done it for some wise and kind, though to us mysterious, purpose."[21] In this understanding, God is powerful and good, in charge and immutable. God's actions are mysteries only to us in our weak faith and shallow understanding. Contrast this with a more recent discussion by Martin Marty of the death of the daughter of a friend. Tacey Louise Rehkopf, driving on her way to college in September 1983, was killed when a leaf spring broke off from a truck, flew in the window of her car, and killed her. Where the nineteenth century simply assumed that everything that happened was the will of God (a position that persists, as we have already seen), Marty confesses lack of knowledge about that. He quotes from her father's remarks at Tacey's memorial service:

We would be less than loyal to her high, humorous, joyful faith if we did not now acknowledge and carry on that same faith within ourselves....I give you a story about five-year-old Tacey: When JoAnn and I took her and a loved cousin, Martha, to see Martha off for home after a happy summer visit, Tacey knew that we saw tears about her, as the train pulled away. "I'm not crying; my eyes are just sweating!" she insisted.

Marty concludes: "Was that leaping leaf spring 'the will of God'? I do not know. Picture, only, the eyes of God, sweating."[22] An immutable God may be easier to grasp intellectually, but such a God is of little help in our suffering. God as sweaty-eyed co-sufferer touches us at our deepest levels. The now-famous story by Elie Wiesel about God hanging on the scaffold in the concentration camp also captures this revised understanding of the character of God.[23] In this approach, we are not invited to yield to the nonrational as the will of God, but to open ourselves to God's presence and the comfort and renewal that can bring.

From beginning to end, the Bible presents to us the possibility of the presence of God. Young Israel sought, awkwardly but persistently, for that presence. Psalmists rejoiced in God's presence and lamented its absence. And Jesus Christ, God-with-us, promised that he would be with us always, to the close of the age. Here is an excerpt from a sermon on Exodus 33 in which I sought to address the importance of God's presence in our lives:

> The children of Israel were camped at the foot of Sinai. They had already received from the hand of God their freedom and a law by which to organize their life together. And it was time to go, time to strike the tent and move out toward the promised land. One thing they lacked. And Moses, perhaps the only person in our history who could quarrel with God and win, was dickering with God about it.
>
> God: It's time for you to go, to go up to the land which I promised to Abraham, Isaac, and Jacob.

Moses: Are you going with us?

God: No, but I'll send an angel with you.

Moses: That's not good enough.

God: But if I go with you, I might consume you. You're such a stiff-necked people, I don't think I can stand to be with you.

Moses: If you won't go with us, then don't carry us up from here.

Moses knew that the presence of God with the people was endangered. He knew that without the presence of God they never would have made it out of Egypt, through the waters, across the desert. He knew that without the presence of God they were doomed. And so he ran the most outrageous bluff in history: "If you won't go with us, then we won't go." It was like a minor league pitcher with a losing record holding out for a $10,000,000 contract.[24] It was all at stake in that moment. Was our faith to be couched in a code laid down by an absent God who can't stand us? Or was it to be a faith marked by the presence of God? Is God with us? Or is God gone? There was a pause and then God finally replied, "I will go with you and I will give you rest."[25]

No twentieth-century scholar has done more to help us understand the presence of God than Samuel Terrien. His book *The Elusive Presence* traces our understanding of God's presence through the scriptures. He suggests that the concept of covenant, important as it is, fails to explain the specificity of Israel's religion among the cults of the ancient Near East or the peculiar quality of the Christian gospel within the religious syncretism of the Mediterranean world. So what did explain it? The people whose quest for God gave rise to the Hebrew and Christian scriptures entertained a unique theology of presence.[26] They came to know that God's presence was powerful, beneficent, and elusive. Terrien describes that elusive presence this way:

In biblical faith, human beings discern that presence in a surging which soon vanishes and leaves in its disappearance an absence that has been overcome. It is neither absolute nor eternal but elusive and fragile, even and especially when human beings seek to prolong it in the form of cultus. The collective act of worship seems to be both the indispensable vehicle of presence and its destroyer. Presence dilutes itself into its own illusion whenever it is confused with a spatial or temporal location. When presence is "guaranteed" to human senses or reason, it is no longer real presence.[27]

Terrien is correct. God's presence, though essential to our well-being, is not guaranteed even or especially in church. But I submit that crisis is unusually hospitable to this surging presence that both reassures and redeems.

> God is our refuge and strength,
>   a very present help in trouble.
> Therefore we will not fear,
>   though the earth should change,
>   though the mountains shake in the heart of the sea.
> (Psalm 46:1-2)

> Where can I go from your spirit?
>   Or where can I flee from your presence?
> If I ascend to heaven, you are there;
>   if I make my bed in Sheol, you are there. (Psalm 139:7-8)

The emphasis upon presence continues in the New Testament. Jesus is called Emmanuel, or God-with-us, at the beginning of the Gospel according to Matthew (1:23). His last words in that same Gospel are "Remember, I am with you always, to the end of the age" (28:20). Paul said, "[nothing] will be able to separate us from the love of God in Christ Jesus" (Romans 8:38), and we read in the last chapter of the Bible:

The throne of God and of the Lamb will be in [the city], and his servants will worship him; they will see his face, and his name will be on their foreheads. And there will be no more night; they need no light of lamp or sun, for the Lord God will be their light, and they will reign forever and ever. (Revelation 22:3*b*-5)

This presence which we affirm as saving and glorious inevitably fades from our sight, but Terrien says: "When God no longer overwhelmed the sense of perception and concealed himself behind the adversity of historical existence, those who accepted the promise were still aware of God's nearness in the very veil of his seeming absence. For them, the center of life was a *Deus absconditus atque praesens.*"[28] Even in the veil of absence, God remains near to "those who accept the promise."

3. Promise

This leads to the third theological affirmation, which is essential as we give voice to our faith in crisis: the promise. God's promise, which reverberates through the pages of scripture, is that everything is going to be all right.[29] The problem with that, of course, is that anyone who looks outward at the world or inward at his or her own life knows that everything is not all right. So perhaps God does not understand the gravity of the situation, or God knows but is incapable of doing anything about it, or God knows and is at work to this very hour making good on the ancient promise. I choose the latter because that is my conviction and because it is the only response that offers hope. So how is God at work? The book of Genesis tells the story of creation, beautiful and fair. But with the entry of sin into the world, creation goes awry, and God, surely fatigued with the ongoing work of creation, must now also begin the work of redemption. How?

Years ago I heard a sermon by James Wharton on Gene-

sis 15. God is there making covenant with Abram. The sac-
rificial animals were cut in half. Then, "when the sun had
gone down and it was dark, a smoking fire pot and a flam-
ing torch passed between the pieces" (15:17). Thus, in
Wharton's words, "God walked the bloody path of
promise."[30] The promise, "to your descendants I give this
land, from the river of Egypt to the great river Euphrates,"
is made in the midst of blood and suffering. And it is
worked out in scripture and in life the same way. God's
beloved son, Jesus, walked the bloody path to Golgotha
and paid there the price for the sins of the world. For that
reason, we read in Hebrews, Christ "is the mediator of a
new covenant, so that those who are called may receive the
promised eternal inheritance, because a death has occurred
that redeems them from the transgressions under the first
covenant" (9:15). And what is this "promised eternal inheritance"? According to 2 Peter, the promise is "a new heaven
and a new earth, where righteousness is at home" (3:13).

So our living is toward that promised future of God,
which has been set forth and redeemed in blood. As Ritschl
said, we "hope backward" and "remember forward" that
the promises of God in the past may be fulfilled in the
future. To the question of why God has chosen to enact the
promise in this bloody way, the answer appears to be that
this is the only witness we seem to understand and accept,
stiff-necked sinners that we are. Could not God have tried
to sit down and reason with us, pointing out the way to
truth and righteousness and the consequences of taking the
wrong way? God did. Had Adam and Eve followed the
rules of living in the garden, had the Ten Commandments
been gratefully accepted, God would not have had to walk
the bloody path of promise again and again. But, as we
know, forbidden fruit tastes good, at least for awhile, and
even as Moses was on the mountain talking with God, the
people were building a golden calf to worship. It is not
God's choosing the bloody path to redemption that is sur-

prising; it is God's patience and love, willing to try yet again to save a sinful people.

And when we preach to people in crisis, we need to hold before them the promise of God, the promise that assures us tomorrow will come. God loves us no less when we have made a mess of things or when the sky falls. God did not make us to be "cast as rubbish to the void,"[31] but to love God and enjoy God forever. And that we shall do so is no vapid, vaporous promise, but one cut in blood and tested by fire. Edward Schillebeeckx describes it this way:

> Everything to which the Bible bears witness is directed toward the fulfillment in the future of God's promise, the history of which has been narrated in faith in the Bible. It is possible to express our understanding of the Bible in this way: we should not look back at the Bible, but rather look forward, with the Bible, to a future which is given us to be achieved.... There certainly is a "deposit of faith," but its content still remains, on the basis of the promise already realized in Christ (realized in fact, but nonetheless still really a *promise*), a promise-for-us, with the result that interpretation becomes oriented to praxis. The Bible reminds us of God's faithfulness in the past, precisely in order to arouse our confidence in God's faithfulness in the future.[32]

A word of caution here: I have spoken of presence and promise in that order for a reason. That God's eternal plan may be hindered but not stopped is a difficult first word for people in crisis to hear. I am writing this section hard on the heels of a funeral for a middle-aged welder who was electrocuted while working on a project in his backyard. The preacher shouted at us that this was *not* an accident, that all of us have a death date inscribed in heaven, and that it was simply the welder's appointed time to die. I find this an odious understanding of who God is and how God works, and an insensitive message to lay upon a grieving family. Present events may seem so overwhelming that to begin by speaking of God's plan and our place in God's future is to risk missing or even alienating our hearers. First, the crisis must be acknowledged. But then, to the admonition to "speak the truth that is in the room," we must go further to "speak the truth that is in the Book," the witness of our faith that God is with us in the midst of the crisis and that God's promise has not been voided by the crisis. Eugene Boring preached it like this:

> By the hospital bed, outside the divorce court, in the midst of the loneliness of another cocktail party, the eyes of our fellow human beings turn to us with questions they dare not even express. We want to say, and sometimes even do say, "Everything is going to be all right." Even Anne Frank wrote in her diary just a few days before their attic apartment was finally discovered by the Nazis and they were all carted off to die at Auschwitz, "I think it will all come out right." What is this we say to each other? At best, trite? At worst, a lie? While we are trying to make up our minds, the song breaks out again. It starts with the four living creatures around the throne, then spreads in concentric circles to the elders, is taken up by the uncountable numbers of angels, and spreads until
>
> > I heard every creature in heaven and on earth and under the earth and in the sea, and all that is in them, singing,
> >
> > > "To the one seated on the throne and
> > > to the Lamb be blessing and honor and
> > > glory and might forever and ever."
> > > (Revelation 5:13)[33]

How did the welder die? We know that. Why did he die? That is harder. But as we struggle with it, we can affirm that God is with us now and forever. One of the most impressive examples of faith in God's promise that I have seen came in a small newspaper article I saw years ago. A woman was taken hostage during a bank robbery. Her abductor constantly threatened to kill her. She was forced to drive a get-away car while the robber and the police exchanged gunfire, and bullets whizzed all over the place. After it was over, she was asked by a reporter if she had been afraid. "At first," she replied, "but after a while, no." "Why?" asked the incredulous reporter. She said, "Because I realized that *ultimately* he could not hurt me." Amen.

CRISES OF DECISION

Sometimes the crises we face emerge not because we do not understand what is at issue, but because we do not know what to do in response. Buttrick says:

> There are moments ... when prereflective acting is impossible because impulses and conventions are in conflict, and postreflective precedents are simply not available. In such moments human beings agonize over decisions; they ask, "What on earth am I to do?"[34]

Whereas crises of theological understanding may call for sermons on remembrance, presence, and promise, crises of decision may require different approaches.

One helpful approach for the preacher is to examine crises of decision through the lens of "pilgrimage."[35] Pilgrimage calls us out of the ruts of ordinary living. So does crisis. If the crisis situation, which has jerked our support system out from beneath us, can be reconfigured into the language of pilgrimage, our people may catch a vision that will help them with the directional decisions they have to make. We can recount for them how pilgrims set out from their everyday lives in quest for God. They had to learn the rules of pilgrimage, the customs and patterns of the trail. They had to discover what was constant and what was subject to change. They had to deal with roadblocks. They sometimes saw their familiar landscape change, or had to change it themselves. They labored in brush-clearing. They became aware of overlooked parts of the landscape. They had to watch for signs of danger and listen to the pilgrimage guides who could recommend good roads and warn them about places where there were robbers, bad water, and so forth. Finally, they had to reflect on the goal of their journey, where they were headed and why. As they say in the Sahara Desert, *garin maganin hanya* ("the town is the cure for the road").[36] Being in crisis can paralyze; being on pilgrimage can energize. Crisis is often experienced as a dead end; pilgrimage can be the way toward God.

Using the rubric of pilgrimage, preachers may then deal with crises of decision as opportunities to get on—or back on—the right road toward God. Energy, hope, and direction become key ingredients. This section offers several ways of approaching that last ingredient, direction. No trajectory in life is without its barriers and washouts. Life can indeed turn on a dime. Straight, clear paths become crooked and murky. If we are *in* crisis, then we want to get *out*. "What shall we do now?" is another way of saying "Where shall we go from here?" or "Which direction shall we take now?" And that of course brings questions of goal or destination into play. As Alice and the cat say to each other:

> Alice: Will you tell me, please, which way I ought to go from here?
> Cat: That depends a great deal on where you want to get to.
> Alice: I don't care where.
> Cat: Then it doesn't matter which way you go.[37]

Not long ago, I attended a prayer retreat in which our director led us in an exercise called the "Prayer of the Six Directions," namely north, south, east, west, up, down.[38] One of the things I appreciated about the prayer was the implication that at different times and places in life, our needs and consequently our prayers are different. Summer (south) is different from winter (north) and so forth.

The exercise suggested that all directions are sacred, that there is nowhere we can go on pilgrimage that God does not go with us. What struck me later, and now prompts these responses to crises of direction, is the truth of this insight—all directions can be sacred; all directions can lead to God. There are always options. And in every situation there is a saving possibility. But it is also true that all directions can lead to perdition. The good or evil of a direction or a road or a choice has to do with more than the compass. It has to do with who and where you are, with your information and understanding, with your faith and your goals; most especially it has to do with what we call ethics.

I am minimally aware of the two major theoretical camps in ethics: the teleological, which emphasizes ends or consequences, and the deontological, which emphasizes the essential *rightness* of certain acts. And I have found myself in both camps. Last summer, a major family decision in our home was made not on the basis of whether it was right or not, but whether it would result in the desired effect two years from now (*goals of the pilgrimage*). In contrast, I had a difficult discussion many years ago with a friend who had abandoned his family. I was not particularly supportive of him. When he asked why, I said, "Because there are some things that a man simply does not do, and one of them is to walk out on his family" (*rules of the pilgrimage*). As a homiletician, I recognize that the shape of these theories corresponds to the homiletical shapes we call inductive and deductive. Both of them can produce good results, as can the ethical theories they often use.

However, most recent works in ethics present the teleological and deontological theories, with their respective weaknesses, and then go on to suggest "a better way." The task of the preacher is not to develop or persuade her or his listeners about the correctness of a particular theory, but rather to open for consideration the biblical and theological bases upon which such theories must stand if they are to be helpful to us. What follows are thoughts about the directions that are available and the issues that are at stake, together with reflections on the question of preaching with these directions and issues in mind. When a crisis of decision or direction envelopes us, where are we to go from here? Borrowing the format of the "Prayer of the Six Directions," here are some thoughts about when it is best to go on, go around, go back, go up, go down, or simply stand still.[39]

1. Go on!

"He set his face to go to Jerusalem"
(Luke 9:51)

Which way shall we go from here? The first answer to that question is generally: straight ahead. The maxim, "The only way out is through," and the advice from Davy Crockett, "Be sure you're right, then go ahead," are popular. Illustrative of this approach is the ubiquitous story of the monk hoeing in the garden who, when asked what he would do if he learned he were to die today, replied, "I would go right on hoeing." Most people in the community of faith are on a more or less good track. When crises derail them, their first thought is to get back on track. What is needed are the necessary skills and the encouragement to do so. Sometimes the problem is not the direction; it is lack of heart or faith or energy. Sometimes a people just run out of gas.

I think that is what happened to the Israelites in Deuteronomy 1. After Moses and the Israelites left Sinai, they headed northeastward across "that great and terrible wilderness" (1:19), until they came to a place called Kadesh-barnea. And there at Kadesh the whole land of Canaan lay before them. Moses said, "See, the LORD your God has given the land to you; go up, take possession, as the LORD, the God of your ancestors, has promised you" (1:21). But apparently they did not. In fact, it has even been suggested that the Israelites spent most of their forty years not in the wilderness, but camped at Kadesh-barnea, just sort of... looking. Every once in a while they sent out spies, and the spies came back with horror stories: "There are giants out there." So the people grumbled and murmured against God and sat.[40] They had been through one crisis after another: leaving Egypt, the Red Sea miracle, the divine encounter at Sinai, the terrible wilderness. The direction ahead of them was clear. But they just could not bring themselves to make the effort.

A people in this situation may not respond to arguments that it is in their best self-interest to go forward. They may have lost interest in their own abilities, their own future, even their own salvation. The needed stimuli are external, a vision of what has happened and can happen again, a vision strong enough to reenergize people for the continuing journey. The best example is Jesus. By the time we reach chapter 9 in the book of Luke, the good days are mostly behind Jesus. He has tried; he has done his best; and it now appears that his efforts have come to naught. Ahead of him lie betrayal, rejection, and death. Was there ever a better time for a person to say, "I'm going on vacation. Don't call me. I'll call you"? But Jesus decides to go on. And to learn from him we must look, not just at his words, but also at his face. "When the days drew near for him to be taken up, he set his face to go to Jerusalem" (9:51).[41] Set his face. *Prosópon estérisen.* What does that mean?

Some years ago I saw Marcel Marceau, the world's greatest mime, in performance. What he could do with his face and the rest of his body was astonishing. He could walk forward and go backward better than Michael Jackson ever dreamed of doing. But the skit that impressed me most was simply called "The Mask." In it Marceau tried on different masks. Each one would leave his face with a particular look until he took it off. He then put on one mask in which his face was set in a sort of silly grin. The only problem was that, when he went to take it off, it did not come. It was stuck. He began pulling, tugging, jumping around, tensing, struggling—but still that silly grin. He was clearly in agony everywhere but his face. When he finally got the mask off, you could see his "real" face: drained, exhausted, relieved. Our faces say a lot about us, and we know that, so we cosmeticize them, nip them, tuck them, and sometimes we make them lie, because we do not want others to know what it is our faces really want to say.

This verse cuts the gospel of Luke in half. The Galilean ministry, that part of Jesus' ministry most like ours—preaching, teaching—the normal ministry of Jesus is over. He will still preach and teach but it will be different and wrapped in an immediacy that colors the content. I once heard Abraham Heschel speak and it was a warm and wonderful presentation. A good time was had by all. I heard him again. He had not long to live, and apparently he knew it. The tenor of the language was different. Even though he spoke conversationally, it was as if he measured every word, every idea, because he might not have the chance to say this, to do this, again. That is Jesus' experience after 9:51. "From now on I will not drink of the fruit of the vine until the kingdom of God comes" (22:18). Jesus and his disciples are clearly on different wavelengths. They are ready to strut their stuff: "Shall we call down fire upon them?" The *Cotton Patch Gospel* parodies their attitude this way: "It's time to take it to the big time, to try out our message at the top."[42] But we do not get that feeling from Jesus. Everything has changed. And it all begins with this line: "He set his face to go to Jerusalem."

Most writers suggest that the phrase simply means "resolute determination." Well, why not say that then? Why the metaphor? Why *prosópon estérisen?* Think about it. Have you ever seen anyone with a face that was set? "Stiffened" in the Greek. Sure you have, and it was not a very pretty sight. Whether it is Marcel Marceau or Queen Victoria with her "We are not amused" or an old-time portrait taken by ambrotype or a beauty pageant contestant or Jesus on the road to Jerusalem—set faces reveal more than resolute determination and conceal more than they reveal.

One possibility is that we set our face to conceal our emotions, to hide our feelings, to keep others from penetrating to the deeper levels of soul and spirit. Our face becomes a mask, forbidding like the Phantom of the Opera or silly like the masks of Halloween. I remember 1964 when I was doing civil rights work in Mississippi. I had only been there a short while and my face was filled with exhilaration, the possibility of change, and fear. But there were others who had been there a long time. As we sat in the Pike County jail I could not help noticing that some of my colleagues' faces had stiffened and the light had gone out of their eyes. They had been idealistic once, years ago. But too much pain, too much suffering, too much death had robbed them of that, replacing their idealism with a kind of grim determination. They would see it through and die if need be, but the joy and the hope were gone, and their faces were set, to hide the emptiness behind them.

Is that what we have with Jesus? Too many nights on the road with no place to sleep, too much rejection, too little understanding, too little change. Is he worn out, washed up, unwilling to give up but anxious to get it over with? Sounds like one of Carmen de Gasztold's prayers from the ark. Do you remember the prayer of the old horse?

> See, Lord,
> my coat hangs in tatters,
> like homespun, old, threadbare.
> All that I had of zest,
> all my strength,
> I have given in hard work
> and kept nothing back for myself.
> Now

my poor head swings
to offer up all the loneliness of my heart.
Dear God,
stiff on my thickened legs
I stand here before you:
Your unprofitable servant.
Oh! Of Your goodness,
give me a gentle death.[43]

Has Jesus, like the old horse, given all he has to give, and now with stiffened face, makes his way to Jerusalem, hoping only for a gentle death, and afraid it is not going to be that way? Best not to show it. No more feelings. No more frowns. No more smiles.

Sometimes we set our faces for exactly the opposite reason: not to hide our suffering or our emptiness, but to hide our joy. Over fifty years ago a woman named Zora Neale Hurston wrote a book about what it was like to be a Black woman in the South, and she called it *Their Eyes Were Watching God*. The main character is a Black woman named Janie. Abandoned by her parents, she is raised by a very controlling grandmother. She is given to one man who abuses her and then to another who belittles her. Finally, this man, her husband, dies, and for the first time in her life, she is not controlled by another person. For the first time in her life, she is free. Janie goes to the funeral, and Hurston writes it this way:

> Janie starched and ironed her face and came set in the funeral behind her veil. It was like a wall of stone and steel. The funeral was going on outside. All things concerning death and burial were said and done. Finish. End. Nevermore. Darkness. Deep hole. Dissolution. Eternity. Weeping and wailing outside. Inside the expensive black folds were resurrection and life. She did not reach outside for anything, nor did the things of death reach inside to disturb her calm. She sent her face to Joe's funeral, and herself went rollicking with the springtime across the world.[44]

Maybe that is what is going on with Jesus. All suffering and death on the outside, but peaceful and calm on the inside. So he starched and ironed his face and sent his face to Jerusalem while he himself went rollicking in the spring-time of heaven. You can set your face to hide your feelings, or the absence of them.

You can also set your face not to say "no more feeling," but rather "no more thinking." "My mind is made up, don't bother me with the facts." "God said it, I believe it, and that settles it." Back during the Depression when there was so much suffering going on, Senator Breckenridge Long said of Herbert Hoover, "He has set his face like a flint against the American government's giving one cent to starving Americans."[45] Does that sound vaguely familiar? How about Isaiah 50? "I have set my face like a flint, and I know that I shall not be put to shame." Some people think that is the source of Luke's description. There is opposition implied here.[46] "I'm not going to think about it anymore. My enemies are God's business, and God will get them." Is that why hard questions about sexuality and the church often go begging for discussion? Because a lot of people just do not want to think about it anymore? After all, "God said it, I believe it, and that settles it."

Could it be that Jesus just does not want to think about it anymore? When he looks ahead of him, is the opposition and the pain he sees so depressing that he just blocks it out, shuts down his neural transmitters, and sets his face like a flint?

Or maybe Jesus' setting his face does not so much mean "no more feeling" or "no more thinking" as it does "no more Mister Nice Guy." No more kissing babies. No more nondirective counseling. There is a considerable scholarly tradition which suggests that Luke takes this phrase not from Isaiah 50 but from Ezekiel 21:

The word of the LORD came to me: Mortal, set your face toward Jerusalem and preach against the sanctuaries;

prophesy against the land of Israel and say to the land of Israel, Thus says the LORD, I am coming against you.[47]

In this understanding, setting your face means judgment against that toward which your face is set, and I understand that. My wife is a school administrator, and she tells me that, just as drill sergeants practice their *command voice*, teachers practice *the look*. I remember Ms. Morrow's *look* in eighth grade. Scared me half to death and kept me on the straight and narrow. We have all felt that look, I suppose. Do you think that is what this is? When Jesus sets his face toward Jerusalem, is Luke telling us less about Jesus and more about Jerusalem and all it represented: "not one stone will be left upon another"? Judgment Day is coming.

No more feeling. No more thinking. No more kindness. There may be elements of all these involved in this image, but I am not convinced. I am not convinced that one who sees Jerusalem and stops on the road to cry is one devoid of feeling (19:41). I am not convinced that one who could engage the Sadducees in a point-counterpoint about the resurrection has stopped thinking (20:27-40). And I am not convinced that one who would gather the little children around him and bless them (18:15-17), one who would tell the people not to worry, that God would take care of them (12:22-31), is one consumed with judgment.

"Jesus set his face to go to Jerusalem." Let me suggest a very simple way to understand this phrase, the journey to Jerusalem, and the passion. *Jesus was ready to do it God's way.* He knew what was ahead of him and what does he say again and again as he lives the days that follow? "Thy will be done. Thy will be done." More than just determination. "Damn the torpedoes. Full speed ahead!" More than that. And more than just resignation. "I've done the best I can, and that's all I can do." More than that. Jesus was ready to see God's plan unfold and to play his part in that plan to the fullest. His attitude differed from that of the disciples in that they were ready to see what they could do (and we know how that turns out!). Jesus was ready to see what God could do.

As I go out among the churches, I see a lot of dedication. I see people who give sacrificially, who rally to the support of those who need help. I see good programming. I see a lot of good things. But I also see a lot of low expectations. I do not think there are many of us who believe that God is about to do something big. I see very little anticipation of the new world that God is bringing into being. We do not seem to *need* anything from God and so we do not *expect* anything from God. And we sure are not getting ready for God to do something big.

Jesus set his face and headed out. This is Luke's travelogue: Jesus on the Passion road. But there is just one thing. It is a lousy travelogue. Have you noticed that? Take a map of the Holy Land and a marking pen and try to follow the trip. It does not work. Has Luke set us up with a false structure to throw in some of his own stuff about Jesus? Or does he use the travel motif to accomplish something else: to draw us into a pilgrimage with Jesus in an unfolding and deepening way?[48] Maybe the journey to Jerusalem that Luke has in mind is ours, maybe he wants us to know that God is about to do something big and that we had better get our *game face* on. In having Jesus set his face toward Jerusalem, ready for God's will to be done, Luke may just be saying to us, "You better get ready."

God may be found more out ahead of us than in any other direction and Jesus has shown us the way: God's way. So when a present crisis threatens to envelope us in darkness, we preachers need to remind our congregations that we are the people of God and God's way is forward. We can then point the way toward God's future, and encourage our people to get up, dust themselves off, and keep walking in the direction which Jesus has led.

2. Go around!

"They left for their own country by another road"
(Matthew 2:12)

Which way shall we go from here? If we do not know, to whom do we look? There is, as John Deschner put it, a serious mistrust of visionaries, of the great system builders, today.[49] In biblical language, there is no frequent vision these days, everyone does what is right—or wrong—in his or her own eyes. Few and foolish are those who attempt systematic theologies. So what is our responsibility as preachers in helping people find good direction in crisis?

The previous section spoke of perseverance, about what it means for us to set our faces toward Jerusalem. When the question is, Shall I press on? the answer is not so much a Crockettian "Be sure you're right, then go ahead," as it is a willingness to proceed God's way. To go on suggests a confidence that God is about to do something that we do not want to miss. Do we believe that? And do we live as if we do?

Now, consider the next question. Should one always "press on toward the mark"? No. Sometimes the way is completely blocked. Sometimes the right way turns wrong. Sometimes the shortest distance between two points is a wavy, roundabout, crooked line.

There are a number of places in scripture where the straightforward approach to an issue is abandoned for a circuitous one. It does not take forty years to get from Goshen to Canaan as a crow flies. But there were reasons. One of the most vivid places where the story goes around instead of straight is in the Matthean birth narrative. If ever there were a setting for straightforward action, one would think that the advent of the Christ would be it. "Put it right out in front of us, God. Let there be no doubt, no misunderstanding." And what do we get? Five changes of direction in the first two chapters, corresponding with five of the six dreams recorded in the New Testament:

1:20—angel appears to Joseph, tells him not to reject Mary.

2:12—magi, warned in a dream, take another road home.

2:13—angel tells Joseph to take Mary and Jesus and flee to Egypt.

2:20—angel tells Joseph to go back to Israel.

2:22—Joseph warned in a dream to go to Galilee.

These whipsaw movements are followed immediately by the coming of John the Baptist, whose task is to "prepare the way of the Lord, make his paths straight" (3:3). This sidebar is either a little joke by the gospel writer ("Straight paths? Jesus? Right....") or wishful thinking ("If anyone ever needed his paths straightened, it is Jesus."). But, either way, Jesus never got the message. Even though Jesus set his face toward Jerusalem, the texts frequently say that when people came to him with specific, straightforward questions, "Jesus spoke to them in parables." "What about this, Jesus?" "Well, a man had two sons ..." "Do you speak to them in parables so they will understand?" "No, I speak to them in parables so they will not understand." Right. Following Jesus can make one dizzy sometimes. The birth narratives present five critical moments in Jesus' life and ours, all involving dreams. I am not so much interested here in psychological approaches to dream theory as I am in the fact that in the Bible, the dream is primarily a form in which God speaks. So what we have in the dreams is a way of saying that the Word of God came to Joseph.

What can we learn? First, the actor in all of these decisive moments is God; the responders are Joseph and the magi. So from this biblical story the first point in changing direction is that God provides the impetus. Deontologically, we know that Joseph's changes of direction are right because God said so. Teleologically, they are right because the goal of saving Mary and Jesus was good.

Second, we also see from this story that, biblically speaking, a change of direction or repentance, is always beyond human powers. From the prophets to our own twelve-step programs, we realize that. Joseph could not have come up with these good and brilliant maneuvers on his own. So scripture warns us, with Joseph, about our need for change and the impossibility of our doing it alone.

So far, so good. But now the situation gets tough. Probably the most famous rendition of this text is Rembrandt's painting. Mary sits beatifically in the stable. Joseph is off to her left, leaning on his staff, asleep. The angel is just behind Joseph, touching his left shoulder with one hand and pointing with the other. "Wake up, Joseph. Take Mary and the child and go in this direction." You soon notice that the angel is not in front of Joseph, beckoning, "Come this way." This is not Hopeful calling back encouragement to Christian as they ford the Jordan in Bunyan's *Pilgrim's Progress*. This is not Jesus going on ahead preparing both the way and a place for us. And this is not the process God luring us on. Joseph's situation is not that easy. There is no assurance that the angel will either lead or accompany; no guarantee that all will be well. What the angel gives is impetus and direction, a hand on our shoulder (or a swift kick) and a finger pointing the way. My friend Bryan Feille says that in his experience most people want change but they really do not want *to change*. They want to be thin but are not willing to pay the price of diet and exercise. They want a better marriage but are not willing to change the patterns of behavior—destructive as they may be—that they have grown comfortable with. Most people, he says, change not because they want to but because they have to, because something clobbers them: a tornado, a death, a job loss, an angel.

Pastor Martin Pike once wrote in his church newsletter about angels and said that they must be instructed early in their training to begin each conversation with "Be not afraid." And that is a good thing, Pike says, because what they generally do after they say "Be not afraid" is tell us to go somewhere or do something that we are afraid to do. "Angels," in his words, "can be kind of pushy."[50]

They can, indeed. With angels it is push, not pull, and that is always harder. But sometimes it is all we have. The direction is general, not specific. Intermediate goals are unclear. We must act with partial information. We are propelled but not dragged, because we are free. We know we should change directions, go a different way, repent, because God said so. We know the direction in which we should go, because God said so. But how are we going to get there? How are we going to get around this massive roadblock, this sin, this alcoholism, this depression? The best answer I can muster is that this is when we really need a friend. I have never heard a sermon on the relationship between Mary and Joseph, but I would like to someday. These constant, wrenching changes that they went through—how much harder those would have been if they had not had each other.

And this is where those of us who want to be Jesus' friends come into the picture. This is why we have church and ministry. People come to us blocked; they can no longer press on toward the high mark of their calling. Most often they come to us not because God has not acted, not because they have not been shown the way, but precisely because God has acted and pointed them in the right direction, and they cannot get there. They are frozen by fear, loneliness, pain.

So how can we help? By remembrance, presence, and promise. We can walk with them, recall for them the faithfulness of God, help them to better listen for the word of God in their lives, and describe the playing field ahead of them—pointing out paths and pitfalls. Stanley Hauerwas suggests that the best ethic is neither deontological nor teleological, but narrative. We make decisions based on the kind of people we are. And we can help people strengthen themselves into the kind of people who make better decisions. How many examples of this have we seen? James

Fenhagen suggests, "We have a direction, but no road map. And we are more than wanderers; we are pilgrims."[51] Bilbo Baggins also says in *The Hobbit*, "I am terrified of the journey. But I have friends."[52] Our help can become a witness as it shapes our own life and personality, helping others beyond the immediate situation. How do the people answer in El Salvador, when the roll call of the martyrs is read name by name? "Presente."

To summarize. All directions lead to God, but all do not lead there directly. One of the more difficult decisions we face is that of taking a road other than our present one. Biblically speaking, the impetus and the direction for change come from God. But the courage and help that we need for the daily walk must come from God's friends and ours, the church. God has no feet but ours to walk the walk of faith with one another.

3. Go back!

"When Micah saw that they were too strong for him,
he turned and went back to his house."
(Judges 18:14-26)

Which way shall we go from here? John Muir (1838–1914) was America's greatest naturalist and mountaineer. Once he was climbing Mount Whitney in late autumn. Although a snowstorm descended and Muir was without a blanket in temperatures reaching twenty-two degrees below zero, he pressed on, obsessed with reaching the summit. Survival did not matter; only the summit. He struggled to within five hundred feet of the top. Suddenly, he said, "I felt as if Someone caught me by the shoulders and turned me around forcibly, saying 'Go Back' in an audible voice."[53] Sometimes the prophetic word in a crisis is stop, turn around and go back.

Here is a story from the book of Judges, in case you have not come across it recently in your devotions. There was a young man named Micah from the hill country of Ephraim. He stole some silver from his mother, but finally confessed and returned it. She was so pleased by his repentance that she gave him part of the silver to set up his house. He did, made an idol of part of the silver, and hired a priest. But the Danites, rough fellows who were looking for a home, descended on Micah's house, stole his idol and his priest, and went their way. When Micah discovered this, he summoned a posse and went after them, braver in this case than he was smart. He caught up with the Danites and the following dialogue ensued:

> [Micah and his men] shouted to the Danites, who turned around and said to Micah, "What is the matter that you come with such a company?" He replied, "You take my gods that I made, and the priest, and go away, and what have I left? How then can you ask me, 'What is the matter?'" And the Danites said to him, "You had better not let your voice be heard among us or else hot-tempered fellows will attack you, and you will lose your life and the lives of your household." Then the Danites went their way. When Micah saw that they were too strong for him, he turned and went back to his home. (18:23-26)

This story raises many questions, not the least of which is what it is doing in scripture. Given the Hebrew penchant for telling their own stories, even when the stories were bad, if there were lessons to be learned, we can guess. We can surmise that religious faith cannot be made or bought, as Micah tried to do, nor can it be achieved by force, for the Danite's worship center did not last long.

The part that intrigues me is Micah's reaction after his gods and his priest were stolen. That was not right, so Micah rode after the Danites. What happened was similar to what happens to the cartoon character Calvin when he goes after Moe, the class bully. What do you do when you catch him? You turn back and go home, lucky to be alive.

I think perhaps part of the reason for this story rests in the second line of Reinhold Niebuhr's famous prayer: "God grant me the courage to change what I can, the serenity to accept what I cannot change...." There are some times when the goal, as wonderful as it may seem, is unattainable, or only attainable at such a cost as to make it undesirable. And we need to know, in the words of the country song, "when to fold 'em," when to turn around like Micah and go home.

One of the hardest things that many of us have to learn in ministry is when to give up. Many of us have left the ninety and nine to go after the one, which is good. But we may then end up spending so much time with the one that the ninety-nine fall apart. Many of us have pushed programs and ideas that the people would not accept until finally our relationship was destroyed and we had to leave. "We shall never surrender" may have been good words coming from Churchill, but they are not always wise coming from a minister. If "Go on" is about persistence and "Go around" is about discernment, then "Go back" is about submission.

We could go to a lot of saints and mystics for guidance here, for an answer to Micah's dilemma and mine and probably yours. Francois Fenelon said that when God teaches us to die to ourselves, God touches our tenderest part, for there we are most sensitive and weak. We should fix our attention upon God. Silence, peace, and communion with God will compensate us for all the injustice we suffer.[54]

Good counsel. But sometimes the words of the old saints are more frustrating than they are helpful. Let me rather tell you the story of a new saint, an American named Tom Kelly, who died at the young age of 47, during World War II.

Kelly was a student of Whitehead with a fierce and passionate devotion to scholarship. An excellent teacher with a profound spiritual life, he was faced with two crises in the late 1930s: declining personal health and a darkening world. Kelly traveled to Germany for the American Friends

Service Committee and saw the gathering storm. He came home depressed and took a vacation. Finally he wrote back to his friends in Germany these words:

> As the clouds sink lower, I am often with you all in prayer. We have spent most of our vacation here in Maine, deep in the fir woods on the ocean.... It's a very primitive life and we are *forced* to live close to nature.... We have the use of a sailboat and find joy in seeing how [our wishes] and the winds have to work together. It is good to bow before the forces of nature as well as to conquer them. The spirit of our time lays such emphasis on the conquering, the activity; I find that we also learn from listening, waiting, helpless expectancy.... In the end no one is free till [that one] has experienced the wonderful slavery of the chains of divine love.[55]

Kelly said, "I am going to make my life a miracle." And he did. He did not stop World War II. He did not make a great contribution to his academic field. He submitted himself to God, and waited. What he produced in the two years he had left in this world was a series of articles later published as *A Testament of Devotion,* one of the most helpful guides to spiritual living since Brother Lawrence's *Practice of the Presence of God.*

So what can we say about direction today? To go forward is to be ready for God's will to be done, but when the word comes irrevocably to go back, the message is almost always that we have been going in our way and not God's, even though our way has seemed good.[56] Sometimes we have arrived at our way with great devotion and care, believing that our way is the best way not only for us but for those given into our care. And having to give that up can be a source of great pain.

To turn around and go back—humiliated, discouraged, and angry—is a wonderful opportunity. It is hard to write that sentence with a straight—or "set"—face; it may be even harder to read it that way. I believe it intellectually, but it is not easy to believe at a visceral level and even more difficult to convince others. We run the risk here of having a significant biblical truth trivialized into a "turn your scars into stars" approach to dealing with adversity. The problem again is one of works-righteousness in which we replace one bad direction of ours with another that we hope will be better.

Every one of us can remember some time when we were badly treated, humiliated, and left seething with anger. Micah's abject humiliation at the hands of the Danites surely left him angry, bitter, and helpless. What he did not realize is that those things stolen from him, a cast metal god and a hireling priest, were not good for him, were perhaps deadly for him and for his soul. Sometimes we have to go back, either because the way was not good for us or the goal was simply unachievable. It takes a lot of courage to admit that we were wrong, to submit our wills to God's, or simply to recognize that some of our goals may not be accomplished because God intended them for others.

One night not long ago I worked late at school and was driving home about midnight when my headlights picked up an animal on the road. I slowed down, and as I approached, I saw that it was a coyote, frozen in the middle of the road by my lights. I pulled over, turned my lights off, and got out. They coyote trotted over to a grassy area, and then we just stood, staring at each other in the moonlight. There was no doubt that it was a coyote, right in the middle of town, some five miles, as I figured, from open country.

Was it Bob Dylan who said, "One should not be where one does not belong"? That coyote did not belong there. Whether or not he had been driven there by hunger or illness, through parks and vacant lots, along creeks or parkways—if he stayed, he was going to die. This was our turf, and he was a threat to pets and small children. I tried to think of some way I could help him, but there was none. I could not open the door to the pickup and say, "Here, nice doggie, doggie. . . ." I had to call the animal control people—my concern for my neighbors meant that—and they would not discuss shrinking habitat or environmental impact with him, they would kill him. So I saluted him as a fellow creature and drove away with this thought in mind: that coyote has one chance and one chance only to survive; he has to find his way out of this place the same way he found his way in. We like to say "the only way out is through" and other forward-looking cheers, such as "press on"; "attack!"; "the best defense is a good offense"; and *"l'audace, toujours l'audace!"* (boldness, always boldness!). But there was no question of *through* here. Survival for that coyote meant *go back*, retreat, and most of all, remember. Remember where you belong, the way you came, and the way back.

Sometimes, it means the same thing for us. When we are lost and confused, sometimes our remembering can remind us of our identity, of who we are, of where we belong. Sometimes, like the prodigal son, we need to find our way back through the detritus of our lives to original ground, where we can find ourselves and take our bearings on the future once again. Being in church on a Sunday morning can literally save our lives. I said earlier that the opposite of *remember* is not *forget*. The opposite of *remember* is *dismember*. Sacred memory re/members us, puts us back together, heals us, and makes us whole. When Christian loses hope of ever reaching the celestial city in *Pilgrim's Progress*, Hopeful reminds him, "Did we not see from the Delectable Mountains the gate of the city?"[57] And if we saw it once, we can see it again.

4. Go up!

"After this I looked, and there in heaven a door stood open!
And the first voice ... said, 'Come up.'"
(Revelation 4:1)

Which way shall we go from here? Caught in the maelstrom of crisis, sometimes we are desperate to reach higher ground. The call to "come up" is clearly heard. Whether through prayer, meditation, vision, or retreat, we seek to escape the burden of our trouble, if but for a while. Engagement with this world can be wearying. During the plagues of the fourteenth and fifteenth centuries, when life was nasty, brutish, and short, the desire to get to God, temporarily or permanently, became all-consuming for many Christians. In today's world some see prayer as escapist and unreal. But, as Parker Palmer makes clear, *escape* is a very necessary part of vital living. He says:

> Escape and engagement are complementary rhythms, not exclusive choices. They ebb and flow, wax and wane, each movement responding to the tugging of the other.... The returned escapee is:
> (1) "better able to deal with those feelings of insignificance,"
> (2) "less likely to faint or grow weary in the face of frustration,"
> (3) "less surprised by evil, and"
> (4) "less likely to founder on the rocks of ego."[58]

In Revelation 4 we see a vivid example of such an escape. In the Spirit on the Lord's Day, John looked up and there in heaven stood an open door, and a voice said to him, "Come up!" John accepts the invitation. What does he see? And what assurances do we have as a result?

First, the door is open, good news to those who need the presence of God. Second, what is it like? A place of splendor, peace, and covenant. Third, there is a throne, and more important, there is Someone on the throne! The universe has not been left to its own devices. Fourth, in God's hand is a book, which is John's way of saying that God holds the future. And finally, God is made visible in the Lamb. Christ is the true witness of God.

What marvelous good news! We are not alone. There is Someone on the throne. The God of peace holds the future and is made known through Jesus Christ. Everything is going to be all right. Our journey up from this world, like John's, allows us to return with stronger hearts to face what is before us, knowing that we do not have to face it alone.

5. Go down!

"Then the LORD said to Moses, 'Go down
and warn the people ...' "
(Exodus 19:21)

Which way shall we go from here? We know a great deal about Exodus 20. And we should, because that is where the Ten Commandments are found. But we know very little about Exodus 19. Exodus 20 is about the content of a theological and ethical system. Believe this. Act this way. Do not believe that. Do not act that way. But Exodus 19 provides the necessary prior action, the landscape in which that content, that theology, that ethic, and that faith can be heard. Exodus 20 gives God's word to the people. But Exodus 19 gives God's word to the person who is going to give God's word to the people. It is God's word to us one step removed. In chapter 19 Moses goes up the mountain four times and every time God tells him: Go down to the people, go down to the people, go down to the people, go down to the people.

I am very Kazantzakian. Nikos Kazantzakis (1886–1957) was a great human being and a great writer who has been one of my heroes for over thirty years. Perhaps his greatest theme was the ascent, the constant, eternal struggle to climb higher in quest for God. I believe in the ascent. I believe in climbing higher, reaching as far as we can and beyond, and I wanted to end this section with that. But we are more than climbers, we are ministers. Therefore I suggest, perhaps to the reader's disagreement, that the ultimate direction is down.

In a three-storied universe that would be damning, but I do not believe in that. What I do believe is that every time somebody in the Bible climbs the mountain to get to God, whether it is Moses or Elijah or Jesus, the message that they receive is "go down." Why? There are surely several reasons.

1. Down is where the earth is, and in the midst of the quest for heaven sometimes we forget how inextricably our lives are bound up with this planet. The planet is not here for us to use up in our quest for the stars. It is our home. When on retreat we offered our Prayer of the Six Directions, and came to *down*, we stretched out flat upon the earth because we belong here. It is where our heritage is, where our history is. Eugene Lowry has told a story about a parsonage being constructed on the other side of a cemetery from its church. In the excavation they unearthed bones, which research told them were slave bones from the period before the Civil War. When he had heard about this from the pastor as they sat in the study of the parsonage, Lowry had asked, "How can you prepare a sermon, fix dinner, even sleep...with all those bones just a few feet below?" Then he answered his own question: "We all do."[59]

Yes. We all do.

2. Down is where the people are. The people do not live on the mountaintop. And this is what makes chapter 19 perhaps more important than its more famous neighbor. God's constant instruction to Moses to carry messages down to the people marks a change in the religious development of the people. Until now, religion has been a hierarchy. Henceforth it shall be a covenant. Not just a law, but a life, a life in which God is present. Samuel Terrien writes that presence is that which creates a people. Presence is the reality to which we must attune ourselves, because there is no solitary life.

God's presence manifests itself in many ways and may be found by journeying in many directions, but the key is this message received at Sinai, and graphically revisioned on a cross against a darkening sky: "I did not just bring you out of Egypt. I did not just send you a messiah. I brought you toward myself."

3. Now a word about the action God commands: "Go down and warn the people." The ministry is more than a ministry of presence and affirmation. Tough love can require a prophetic "no." Go down and warn the people. Think with me again about the Rembrandt painting previously mentioned. There is the angel, standing slightly behind Joseph, with a hand on Joseph's shoulder, with a gentle persistent message, "Wake up, Joseph, take Mary and the baby and flee." When Joseph awakens, he will not see the angel, because of the position, but he will see what the angel sees. When God sends you down like God sent the angel, remember that. The point is not confrontation, the point is not give me the credit, the point is wake up, look and see. And remember this: Joseph has pondered the gospel, Mary has pondered the gospel, the angel has pondered the gospel; we have pondered the gospel. But the angel has pondered something that Joseph and Mary and we have not: Herod.[60] The angel knows how fragile is the good and how powerful the evil. The angel understands the role of singing *gloria* and the role of warning people about Herod. And so must we.

4. This leads to the final reason for the movement down. Down is where our weakness is, our failure, and our vulnerability. And that is where we want to be available to people, even as we go mountain climbing. For the greatest danger in mountain climbing is falling down. We, who know what it feels like to fall down, are called to ministry with other stumblers, that we might better serve the One "who is able to keep you from falling, and to make you stand without blemish in the presence of [God's] glory with rejoicing" (Jude 24).

6. Be still

"... and having done everything, to stand firm."
(Ephesians 6:13)

Where shall we go from here? There is one final answer to that: nowhere. One of the greatest homileticians of our century is an African American man named Henry Mitchell. He has done more than anyone to help all of us to understand and appreciate Black preaching. Recently a festschrift was published in his honor, and Martha J. Simmons wrote this:

> In the 1940s, while on a train ride with students and his wife, Mitchell was asked to move from a train car because it contained White passengers. Since the area of the train reserved for [Blacks] was quite full and ... since there were very few White passengers, Mitchell refused to move. The porter left and returned with a sheriff who waved a large gun in Mitchell's face and said, "Move!" At that moment, Mitchell says, "I decided, as I looked at my wife who was pregnant with our first child, I'll see this child in heaven first, before I'll move from this seat."[61]

Sometimes you just do not go anywhere at all. No one likes to be told to sit still, to be patient, especially in crisis. There is a powerful impetus to do something, to do anything! Frequently, alas, such impetuous action has disastrous consequences. A minister once said to me when I was in crisis, "When you don't know what to do, don't do anything."[62] I despised that advice, but it was not as bad as I thought it was. We have a young friend who returned home to discover that, in a drive-by shooting, gang members had barely missed killing his baby sister. In a rage he got a gun, went looking for them, and in a tragic accident, ended up killing a child. We grieve for the child, for our young friend, and for their lost futures. How much better for all it would have been if, in response to crisis, he had done nothing.

Sometimes, the crisis is so overwhelming that any thought of moving immediately in a creative direction is preposterous. On those occasions, the best, the very best, we may be able to do is sit still, like Mitchell or, if we can, to get to our feet and stand there. Nikos Kazantzakis called his self-study[63] *Report to Greco* and shaped it as a report of his life to his Cretan "grandfather," Domenikos Theotokopoulos, better known as the artist "El Greco." He closed his work this way:

> [One night, Grandfather, you said to me] "There are three kinds of souls, three kinds of prayers. One: I am a bow in your hands, Lord. Draw me, lest I rot. Two: Do not over-draw me, Lord. I shall break. Three: Overdraw me, and who cares if I break! Choose!"

> I chose. Now the twilight casts its haze upon the hilltops. The shadows have lengthened, the air has filled with the dead. The battle is drawing to a close. Did I win or lose? The only thing I know is this: I am full of wounds and still standing on my feet.[64]

Full of wounds and still standing on his feet. Like the welfare mother evicted from her tenement apartment. Like the paralyzed victim of a drunk driver "standing" tall in a wheelchair. Like the machinist laid off from the only job he has ever known. Like the pastor who has been told to look for another church. Like Jesus before Pilate.

The finest treatment of this that I have ever seen is Albert Pennybacker's interpretation of Ephesians 6:13, "Therefore take up the whole armor of God, so that you may be able to withstand on that evil day, and having done everything, to stand fast." Here is the closing section of his sermon entitled "What to Do When You Don't Know What to Do Next":

> So, finally, when we know that evil is real in its power to frustrate, when we know that we need to change from our cleverness to God's armor and that the preparations are going to last, when we see that we are at the right place and in the right fight—then we come to the last guidance of faith when we don't know what to do next. The words are given: "And having done all, to stand."

These are the last admonitions of faith. "Having done all ...": that is a pretty inclusive phrase. To do "all" is a very great amount indeed. It carries with it the notion of having made our very best offering, of having used our very best wisdom, of having attempted our very best plans, of having shared our best aspirations and used every ounce of human power—and still being faced with more than we can overcome, with more than our strength can transcend, with the ways of evil still prevailing until, in all honesty and freed of all self-pity, we simply do not know what to do next. Then we hear the words: "And having done all, to stand."

We have shifted into another new key. We are in a higher key of faith than when we started out. No longer is the question what we can do; for we know there is nothing to do. No longer is there a question about self-blame or human error; for it is too late for all that. We are in faith simply ready to stand our ground, not in belligerence but in conviction; ready to stand watch if that is what it means, ready to face all that evil may bring, wearing the armor of God, but fully knowing that even the best armor may not be adequate for self-preservation. Simply, quietly, the last great witness of faith in the face of evil is the witness of simply standing.

And in that witness we begin to reflect the stance of Jesus himself. I went back and read again the passages that deal with the trial and condemnation of Jesus. At several points we read a pointed little verse like this: "But he was silent and made no answer." That was when the religious court was trying him. Or again, "But Jesus made no further answer ..."; that was when Pilate was interrogating him. "Having done all, to stand."

That's what we do, at last, when we don't know what to do next. We have done all our doing and now we are cast upon our being. We stand. We stand in the confidence that God is faithful. We stand in the humility that knows that our strength is rather puny at best, but God's strength is not. We stand in the knowledge that arguing the point finally is inappropriate, and the debater must be silent. We stand in the faithfulness that knows that our standing can become useful to God, in ways we know not how.

And so we stand, just as Jesus finally, quietly stood. Evil may work its final, horrid frustration and make its inroads and count its victories, but we stand, at last, in the faith that even out of death comes resurrection.

The word of faith for the living of these days is in part the verse: "Therefore take the whole armor of God, that you may be able to withstand in the evil day, and having done all, to stand."[65]

A good word fitly spoken.

Let me sum up these six directional options like this: Which way shall we go from here? On one level, the question does not work, because the chances are good that, when that decision comes, you will not have a choice. Up, down, in, out, forward, back, left, right, east, west, north, south, stationary—the world will probably decide for you. But on another level, the question is critical. Which way shall we go from here? Toward God. The best final answer to the question of direction is this: "If you seek God, then even if you fall, you will fall toward God."

Toward God. Toward God. What then do we preach in crisis?

When the need is to go on: energy and encouragement.

When the need is to go around: wisdom and discernment.

When the need is to go back: memory and hope.

When the need is to go up: prayer and openness.

When the need is to go down: love and dedication.

When the need is to stand: quiet faith.

Chapter Four

WORSHIP AND PREACHING IN CRISIS

ost crisis preaching occurs in the context of worship. David and Paul Duke suggest that "the context of worship itself can become a context for addressing pain."[1] This presents both possibilities and problems to the preacher or, to follow the dual nature of the Chinese character for crisis, dangers and opportunities. Here are a few of the opportunities afforded crisis preaching in the context of worship, along with their attending dangers, followed by an attempt to extrapolate some lessons.

WORSHIP AS SANCTUARY

We may no longer literally grab the horns of the altar to seek safety from our enemies, but the feeling persists: we are safe here. Our world may be falling apart outside, but everything is OK inside. This is not a rational conclusion, since we know that worship is a radically dangerous activity. Nikos Kazantzakis recounts: "Once there was a rabbi who always made his will and tearfully bade farewell to his wife and children before he went to the synagogue to pray, for he never knew if he would emerge from the prayer alive."[2] Worship is not only consuming; it also can be rejected. In Isaiah 1:15 God reminds those with blood on their hands, "When you stretch out your hands, I will hide my eyes from you; even though you make many prayers, I will not listen." And yet, in spite of the dynamic and dangerous character of worship, there is a palpable, compelling attraction to worship in times of crisis. There is a need for The Holy and for holiness in crisis which worship offers as do few other actions.[3] Like the people in the story that opened this book, I thought first, after hearing the news of John F. Kennedy's assassination, of going to church. A few friends and I had seen Kennedy earlier that morning and were still basking in that experience when the news from Dallas came. Everything stopped. After I pulled myself away from the television, what little movement I could muster was toward church and worship. In Ellis Nelson's words, the worshiping congregation is the "habitat of the Spirit,"[4] and there is no sanctuary this world can provide equal to that of God's people gathered in worship, sheltered by the Spirit:

> What a fellowship, what a joy divine, leaning on the everlasting arms;
> What a blessedness, what a peace is mine, leaning on the everlasting arms.
> Leaning, leaning, safe and secure from all alarms;
> Leaning, leaning, leaning on the everlasting arms.[5]

WORSHIP AS FAMILIAR

When one comes to worship, the place, the time, the action, and most of the people, all tend to be familiar. The benefits of this are readily apparent. William Willimon writes: "By providing a patterned, purposeful, predictable way of behaving in the midst of crisis, by symbolically focusing our attention upon norms, beliefs, and sentiments regarding our ultimate concerns, religious ritual gives us a way through crises that might otherwise overwhelm us."[6]

The congregation at worship seems an ideal setting for dealing with crisis: the reassurance of familiar space and symbols, the comfort of the recurring rhythms of the service, the solid theological grounding, the blessing of the arts, and the consolation of mutuality are present. However, the very incongruity of the unfamiliar (crisis) spliced into the familiar (worship) may result in rejection rather than integration. The very arrhythmia of crisis may clash with the rhythm of worship. And all of us know of people who could not come into the place of worship after losing a spouse or child, because being there evoked memories of worshiping with one now absent through death or divorce, and the memories were too painful to bear. Or people may be so angry at God that the very thought of worship is repugnant. One cannot therefore assume that people will always want to be in worship during crises or that they will automatically find the setting and process meaningful.

Willimon, citing anthropologist Edward Norbeck's distinction of two types of rituals in primitive societies, suggests these rituals have counterparts in contemporary churches: "These are *crisis rites* that occur during important times in the community (birth, death, puberty, war, famine) and *cyclic rites* that are periodically repeated for the maintenance of group life (regular cultic gatherings, memorial days, feast days)."[7]

This might be ideally so, but it does not quite work in actuality. We can see that Willimon's *crisis rites* include both developmental (birth, puberty, death) and situational (war, famine) crises. And although contemporary churches may indeed have rites that have become attached to developmental crises (the blessing of infants, baptism or confirmation, memorial services), I have never been part of a church that had a liturgy for war or famine (which is not to say that there have not been times when we needed one!). This adds one more problem to the burden of the minister seeking to lead worship and preach in crisis: the lack of available models for both the service and the sermon.

WORSHIP AS HELP

Fosdick reminded us that "people do not come to church because they are dying to find out what happened to the Jebusites."[8] We come out of joy, out of duty, out of missional concerns, but mostly we come in quest of help: help to come closer to God, to find ways to live better lives, or simply to make it through another day. We come because, as one person said, people are bad enough to need God, but good enough to recognize their need of God.[9] Edward Shils writes:

> Ritual is part of a complex act of self-protection from destructive, unintelligible, and immoral forces. By re-enacting contact with sacred things and reaffirming the rightness, ritual reinforces the beliefs which enable the actor to confront and deal with crises with some anticipation of effectiveness.[10]

Worship allows us, then, by placing ourselves in the presence of God and the community of God's people, to reinforce our shaky faith and draw strength from God and one another. We *re-enact* our faith; that is to say, worship is active. We do something. And when mental systems fail, acting out our faith can sustain us in crisis, even lead to renewed understandings. In Fred Craddock's words, "acting like a Christian can lead to becoming one."[11]

The problem here is the *reflexive* nature of worship. Colbert Cartwright has suggested that worship is reflexive because "it is in giving that you receive; it is through opening oneself toward God that God comes afresh into your life.... God mirrors back to us that love we send forth to [God]."[12] As attractive as this idea may be, it puts the burden of worship on the worshiper. And in crisis, people may be unable to open themselves, may have no love to give. Worshiper-dependent worship may not provide the help people need.

WORSHIP AS WITNESS

"Church is where the gospel becomes credible."[13] Further, "preaching is woven into the dramatic structure of ... worship, which itself is a witness to the gospel."[14] Questions about God and God's relationship to the world are often treated with benign neglect until crises come. And then we sense that the affirmations of faith only make ultimate sense within the community of faith.[15] The primary work of that community is worship, so in the worship of the church our doctrines are taken out, dusted off, examined, reshaped if necessary, and applied. The worshipping community can play at least three roles for those in crisis:

> First, it relieves isolation. Second, it holds up the symbols of our faith so that they are available to us in the time of trauma, symbols such as the Exodus and Resurrection, not to obscure death and pain, but to show that these are not the last word. Third, the community of faith mediates the healing word by receiving our pain and loss and looking to a "further word of meaning."[16]

Worship is that activity which witnesses to us that our beliefs can be trusted. It is essential in ordinary time and in crisis. That many Christians down through the centuries have paid with their lives for the right to worship witnesses to that witness. What is the rationale for worship as witness? Perhaps this: One way of describing worship is as the ongoing prayer, proclamation, and life of Jesus Christ.[17] And Jesus Christ has earned the right to speak! In his magnificent crisis sermon "But When Life Tumbles In, What Then?" Arthur John Gossip said: "We will listen to Jesus Christ: for he spoke from the darkness round the Cross. We mayn't understand Him, or agree with Him, or obey Him: but nobody can challenge His right to speak."[18] As we have seen, it is not easy to worship in crisis. But it is often impossible to endure and overcome crises outside the community of faith and worship. Who is there to listen to, who has a greater right to be heard than Jesus?

WORSHIP AS PRAYER

"Worship is prayer.
And prayer is everything we do in response to God."[19]

Worship as prayer is not a new concept, but it is an important one. When we are in trouble, we turn to God. In Don Saliers' analysis of liturgy as prayer, he speaks of four interconnected strands of prayer: liturgy as praising, thanking, blessing; invoking and beseeching; lamenting and confessing; and interceding.[20] All these modes of prayer, he says, work in relation to one another. But, I suggest, if my experience in worship is in any way typical, much more time is given to praise, thanksgiving, and blessing (often smarmy and unspecific) than to the other three modes put together. The last three cannot be ignored in crisis. But because beseeching (too much like begging), confessing (mind your own business!), and interceding (who am I to know what you need?) are not comfortable ways to pray, we do not practice them, and we are not very good at them. We have work to do.

PREACHING AND WORSHIP

All of these thoughts about worship provide both comfort and challenge for preaching in crisis. Those people who sit before us as we preach are there because they do not know where else to go, because they are desperate for God's love, and because they hope to find comfort and strength, if not understanding, in the worship of God and the Word of God. Ian Maclaren once gave this advice to preachers: "Be kind, for everyone you meet is fighting a hard battle."[21] This is doubly true in crisis. Many may be barely hanging on or, having let go, in free fall. The wise pastor, sensitive to this, keeps at least three things in mind when structuring the Sunday service:

1. *The usual order of service should probably not be changed.* Omitting the hymns or scripture reading to make way for remarks by the mayor will make the service seem more like a meeting and less like worship, less like what people came for. Yes, receive the offering, however that is done. Some may have no money with them, but that is all right. People need the chance to respond to the affirmation of God's love in crisis, even if it comes only in silent, personal pledge. When Martin Luther found himself in a dangerous thunderstorm, he cried out, "Saint Anne, help me! I'll be a monk." We think that promises made to God under duress seldom endure. I think we would be surprised if we knew the truth of that. The offering prompts us to consider: "God, what would you have me do?" And that is a good thing. I had a friend who founded a house church, one that by design had no building or regular pattern of worship. He told me that one thing he and his people learned in this experiment was that the traditional church does some of the things it does for very good reasons. Regular worship is one of them.

2. *Give attention to the various acts of worship: what they say, how they move and feel.* Choose familiar hymns and texts. Even if your custom is to pray extemporaneously, it is probably a good idea to gather your prayer-thoughts beforehand in the quiet of your study and jot yourself some notes. Have I forgotten to praise, thank, and bless God? Invoke God's presence and petition God's mercy? Voice our confession, lamentation, or confusion? Intercede for those who are suffering? One need not write out the prayer, simply provide some cues for gathering the joys and concerns of the people, so that people might open their hearts and minds to God.

3. Preaching is worship. The interconnectedness of the acts and rationales for worship continue with that affirmation. Quoting John Knox, Willimon affirms, "Unless we conceive of preaching as being itself an act of worship, we miss what is most essential in it and what distinguishes it most radically from other kinds of teaching, religious or secular."[22] It is an act of worship in preparation *and* in delivery.

Geoffrey Wainwright agrees and uses the language of the Eucharist to demonstrate that preaching is "not merely located in the context of worship, but that it is a liturgical act itself."[23] Wainwright sees the task of preaching as parallel to that of the Eucharist; that is, *anamnetic* (remembering), *epicletic* (invoking the Spirit of God), and *eschatological* (pointing toward God's future).[24] Note how this parallels the theological affirmations (from the previous chapter) that preaching makes in crisis: remembrance, presence, and promise!

David Buttrick agrees with Willimon and Wainwright, to a degree. Preaching and worship do belong together, he admits. But "there remains a peculiar, probably unresolvable tension between preaching and worship that we must acknowledge.... [It is a] tension between God's immediate word to us and the regularities of our liturgical praise."[25] What Buttrick says is especially germane to crisis preaching. We may say that we do not want our sermon to increase the tension among those gathered for worship in crisis; God knows there is enough tension already. But we cannot help but do so; it is already there in the tension that exists between preaching and worship. Nevertheless, and here is the grace, this tension may relieve some of the other tensions (dangers) that exist when we worship in crisis. The tensions between safety and danger, familiarity and contempt, brokenness and community, as well as concerns about burdening the overburdened and our lack of worshipping skills, can be interpreted in light of the gospel and perhaps find resolution in the faithful witness of the sermon.

CHAPTER FIVE

CRISIS PREACHING: SOME HOMILETICAL STRATEGIES

iven the wide variety of crisis situations and the psychological and theological questions that accompany them, are there any generally applicable principles that might help us when the time comes to preach? I believe that there are. In this chapter I sketch six of them, beginning with the question of whether or not a crisis exists that needs to be engaged homiletically, and following with five suggestions about what to do when the answer to that question is yes.

DETERMINING WHETHER A CRISIS EXISTS

This suggestion may seem pedantic to the point of silliness. "Of course we are in crisis! Anyone can see that!" Often that is the case, but there are two other scenarios that require mention. First, members of the congregation may feel they are in crisis when the minister does not. Some years ago there was a string of murders of young women in the town where I lived. Police looked for something that might tie the murders together. Finally, it emerged that several of the murder victims had at one time or another been members of the same church. That church was packed the Sunday after the news hit the papers. The pastor ignored the issue that day and in the future, thinking it was not a matter to get the church upset about, certainly not in worship. Did he have a point? Assuredly. Did he miss an opportunity to address some important issues, like the meaning of church membership? Most assuredly. If one picks a certain number of names at random from a church membership roll, what do those people have in common that the same number of people picked at random from the telephone book do not? And if those church people should happen to be murdered, what does that say, not just about the perpetrator or the victims, but also about the church? These are not easy questions, but they are important ones, and ones that people will be asking.

The second scenario happens when the pastor senses a crisis that the congregation does not. One summer, years ago, shortly after becoming the pastor of a church in California, I became very nervous when the treasurer's report indicated we were precariously close to being unable to pay our bills (including my salary!). I was about to declare a major crisis when a wise layman in the church sat me down and pointed out that: (1) income had always been lower in the summer, yet (2) the church had always managed to pay its bills, and (3) cash in the bank was not an accurate assessment of the financial or spiritual strength of the congregation anyway. He showed me the assets of the church, which were considerable, and told me to get on with the business of preaching and tending to the sick and wounded. I yielded to his more comprehensive understanding and shut up.

My assessment of the first scenario is that when the people feel there is a crisis and I do not, I must take their feelings seriously and deal with them in a timely, appropriate way. When people feel their pastor does not take their concerns seriously, trust is eroded, and once trust has been damaged, it is hard to recover. Let me give a homely little example of this that I believe applies in larger situations. We were doing Vacation Bible School in a church I was serving. I noticed one little boy who seemed sad all week. Finally, I asked him if something was bothering him, and he told me that his dog had been run over by a car and killed. He asked me if there were a heaven for dogs. I told him yes, that I believed all of God's creatures were gathered into God's eternal care (I still do). Our procedure that week, during our mid-morning snack, was to invite one of the children to return thanks for our milk and cookies. That morning, when it was time for refreshments, I asked this same boy if he would like to lead our prayer of thanks. He agreed and said, "Dear God, thank you for our milk and cookies, and please help all the dead dogs to come back to life. Amen." While most of the children accepted the prayer as the serious petition that it was, I noticed (and so did the boy) that the adults began to smile, and some to giggle. He looked at me with a pained expression, and I preached a brief extemporaneous crisis sermon right then and there, about God's love and care for all of creation, the gift of life, and the promise of eternal life. It may not have been a particularly good sermon, but I took his concern seriously and responded to it. On a larger scale (if there is one), people are often exercised about issues that I have either resolved in my own mind (such as homosexuality) or do not consider a serious problem (such as so-called "welfare Cadillac" people). I do not rush to the pulpit to address every expression of concern that I hear (not long ago, one group I visited as a preacher took me out to lunch to raise their concern about the "Trilateral Commission" as the greatest threat to world peace). But I do note these as concerns, study them, consider what the larger church is saying, and dialogue with my people about the issues. In response to her members being besieged by other people in the community agitated about the so-called "New Age movement," one pastor wrote recently in her church newsletter:

> There are many legitimate concerns in our community. I don't think this is one of them.... Here is the strength of the

Methodist Church: if New Age and humanism were legitimate threats, I would have been informed about them. The UM connectional system has educated and informed persons in all areas of church and society who study what's going on in the church and world. Here's the strength of the Tarrant Area Community of Churches: if the Methodist Church had somehow missed this "peril," then I would have been informed by the other denominations.[1]

Many such problems can be defused before they reach crisis proportions. Should they, however, reach critical mass in the congregation, one must prepare to address them homiletically.

The second scenario, when I sense a crisis that is not sensed by the congregation, requires some discernment. Gene Garrison helpfully reminds us of the danger of treating every issue as one of impending disaster. Preachers, like the little boy in the fable, can cry "wolf" one too many times. As Garrison says: "Manufactured crises are soon seen for what they are: cheap, sensationalist efforts to attract a crowd. Such imagined crises are easily identified as indications of the preacher's failure to discern the real issues of [our] times."[2] Lest we fall into the trap of manufacturing crises, we may seek the counsel of our people, our colleagues, and other people we trust who know more about the issue than we do. This may help us avoid spending too much emotional, spiritual, and political currency on matters that are of little consequence. This caveat, however: the biblical prophets did exactly what I have just warned against, proclaiming a crisis where the people thought one did not exist.[3] So we must add one additional check: is this an issue of immediate theological concern for the people of God, as attested by the cumulative witness of scripture and tradition, the activity of the Holy Spirit, and portending serious consequences if nothing is done?

NAMING THE MONSTER

We now move to some of the ingredients of the crisis sermon itself. The first suggestion parallels the concerns I have raised about speaking the truth that is in the room and helps both to achieve contact with the people and to boil down the crisis to its essentials. The governing metaphor is one that I have borrowed from an old television series: *Magnum P.I.* In one marvelous episode from that series, Thomas Magnum was left adrift in the ocean, treading water, for two days. At one point a shark appeared and slowly began to circle. Magnum flashed back to his childhood to a conversation he had had with his father. He was having trouble sleeping because of a monster that he had envisioned outside his window. His father asked him about the monster and little Magnum graphically described it. "Oh, yes," his father said, "I know him. That's Herman." They proceeded to talk, not about some vague, ethereal monster, but about Herman, and the boy's fear soon became manageable. Remembering this, Magnum began to talk to Herman, the shark, and after a while, Herman swam away.

The first task of crisis preaching is naming the monster. In *Paradise Lost,* Milton wrote of Adam in the garden. Adam saw "the birds and beasts approaching two by two." "I named them as they passed," he said, "and understood their nature."[4] To name the monsters that terrify our people is both to assure our people that we appreciate the gravity of the situation and also to lay the groundwork for understanding it. Furthermore, in the ancient world there was a belief that naming someone or something gave you power over that person or that thing, a tradition that many believe carries over into the Bible itself. To name the crisis that we face can be a touchstone to understanding it and having power to overcome it. This is sometimes called "the Rumpelstiltskin effect" by modern psychologists.[5] Find the monster's name and its threat is lessened. It also helps us to escape the pitfall of the too-ready identification of tragedy with the will of God, a mistake preachers make too often, and one which compounds the tragedy. I have heard AIDS called God's punishment meted out to homosexuals for their violation of the Levitical code. A wonderful God that is indeed.

After President Kennedy was assassinated, a perceptive professor named Jim Corder gave a lecture with powerful homiletical overtones to all of his classes. I remember it word for word a third of a century later because, as part of his lecture, he named the monster. He said, "We have found the monster that stalks us: presumption. Presumption that our puny perceptions of reality are good and true."[6] I shall not forget that crisis message. In 1984, an African American artist named Kimako Baraka was brutally and senselessly murdered. Her brother Amiri preached her funeral, and in it he said:

> Kimako made the ultimate mistake of wanting to be a creative force in this rotten society. Of being moved by truth and beauty. Of wanting to do nothing so much as dance, to express the rhythm of life as a part of that rhythm.... Kimako's crime for which [she was] destroyed, was wanting to be genuinely human, in spite of the madness that passes as sanity and respectability.... Our failure is that we have not created a context in which life can live, in which creativity can be spared and developed, that we have not built a world in which something wonderful and blessed, Kimako Baraka, could exist, where life would be sacred and protected.... My gentle, fragile sister is dead because we failed to protect her.[7]

In many crises the monster has a name. And if we can find it, we have a handle. And if we have a handle, maybe we can open the door and find a way out. A word of caution: this task can require some theological discernment.

The flash point of a crisis is not always its monster. The crisis may seem to be that we cannot read the hymnbooks because the sanctuary is dark. But the sanctuary is dark because the church has not paid its light bill, and the church has not paid its light bill because of a failure of faithful stewardship. The base problem, then, may be a lack of faith among us. To find our way out of this crisis, that may be where we have to begin.

CREATIVE LAMENTATION

There is no question in my mind that one of the reasons modern men and women face so many psychological problems is that we have lost our ability to lament. Our funerals are often sterile little recitals and our sermons, even in the face of disaster, are feel-good enterprises that ignore that people feel bad—shouting, as it were, "Peace! Peace!" where there is no peace.

I heard my parents talk about that long, slow train that brought the body of Franklin D. Roosevelt from Georgia back to Washington in 1945. I have heard how people gathered by the railroad tracks, how others sat glued to radios, monitoring the progress of the train, and I have seen the haunting photograph of that African American man with the river of tears flowing down his cheek. There is something in lamentation that goes beyond the mere naming of the monster.

Consider the book of Lamentations. Its genius lies in the recognition that there are times when there is no substitute for the question: "Is there any pain like my pain?" Lamentations is a book of terrible beauty and profound insight, one which shows us as clearly as anything I know that the expression of grief and the confession of sin are but a short distance in the economy of God from the expression of hope and the gift of new life.[8] As such, it is well suited for

Christian worship on Maundy Thursday, Good Friday, and Holy Saturday, as well as for other times of fear and grief. But I have never heard a sermon out of Lamentations.

Perhaps the closest thing we have to the kind of creative lamentation for which I am searching is the pastoral elegy. It is one thing to say "The President is dead." It is quite another to say:

> When lilacs last in the dooryard bloom'd,
> And the great star early droop'd in the western sky in the
>   night,
> I mourn'd, and yet shall mourn with ever-returning
>   spring.[9]

In her book *Placing Sorrow* Ellen Zetzel Lambert wrote, "The pastoral elegy... proposes no one solution to the questions raised by death but rather a setting in which those questions may be posed, or better, placed. It offers us a landscape." And this landscape is important, she asserts, "because it can contain pain and suffering.... [It] offers us a vision of life stripped not of pain but of complexity."[10]

Another way of describing the form and function of the pastoral elegy and, similarly, sermons that allow people to lament their pain and unanswered questions is to say that they address crises metaphorically. Remember how Stone said some questions in crisis are *poetic* or *metaphoric* questions. Such questions cannot be answered in propositional language. But they can be placed in a pain-containing landscape within metaphors of sufficient size and strength.

One of the significant advantages that the liturgical churches have over the others is the availability of lamentations for use by people in pain, trouble, or fear. I was in a group once in which the leader asked us to list the five things most important to us. The leader then removed them from us one at a time, reducing us to four, three, two, and finally the single most important thing to us in all the world. It was hard. Several people agonized over their choices. Some even attempted to cut the tension with humor, like one woman, called to reduce her list again, who turned to her husband and said, "Well, there you go, honey." There was a monk among us, though, who seemed to be having no problem making his cuts. When, at the end of the exercise, we shared that "single most important thing," he said calmly, "a good liturgy." I was amazed at first. I would never have thought of that. But his response grew on me. A good liturgy that captures in metaphor and rhythm the pathos and persistent hope of people in crisis is a great and wonderful gift.

In 1784 John Wesley wrote:

> I believe there is no liturgy in the world, either in ancient or modern language, which breathes more of a solid scriptural, rational Piety, than the Common Prayer of the Church of England. And though the main of it was compiled considerably more than two hundred years ago, yet is the language of it, not only pure, but strong and elegant in the highest degree.[11]

Consider the prayer of confession from the *Book of Common Prayer.* Vicissitudes of language might cause us to write it differently today. But I doubt we would write it so well.

> Almighty and most merciful Father, we have erred and strayed from thy ways like lost sheep, we have followed too much the devices and desires of our own hearts, we have offended against thy holy laws, we have left undone those things which we ought to have done, and we have done those things which we ought not to have done. But thou, O Lord, have mercy upon us, spare thou those who confess their faults, restore thou those who are penitent, according to thy promises declared unto mankind, in Christ Jesus our Lord; and grant, O most merciful Father, for his sake, that we may hereafter live a godly, righteous, and sober life, to the glory of thy holy Name. Amen.[12]

And is there is a better collect than this one?

> Almighty God, unto whom all hearts be open, all desires
> known, and from whom no secrets are hid: Cleanse the
> thoughts of our hearts by the inspiration of thy Holy Spirit,
> that we may perfectly love thee, and worthily magnify thy
> holy Name; through Christ our Lord. Amen.[13]

In the so-called "free" churches, no such prayers or lita-
nies tend to exist, and it is often up to the preacher to provide the lament for the people, the setting or place or landscape that can contain the sorrow of the people so they will
not have to contain it within themselves forever. Unfortunately, time does not heal all wounds, at least on this side of
the grave. Sadness and pain never lamented but simply
internalized have a way of quietly gathering strength and
someday exploding.

Consider what Walter Brueggemann says about the
lament in Jeremiah, chapters 8 and 9. The text includes such
sad and lovely lines as these, found in verses 8:20–9:1:

> "The harvest is past, the summer is ended,
>   and we are not saved."
> For the hurt of my poor people I am hurt,
> I mourn, and dismay has taken hold of me.
> Is there no balm in Gilead?
> Is there no physician there?
> Why then has the health of my poor people
>   not been restored?
> O that my head were a spring of water,
>   and my eyes a fountain of tears,
> so that I might weep day and night for the slain of my poor
>   people!

Brueggemann writes:

> It is in the embrace of and engagement with the hurt and
> forsakenness of 8:18–9:3 that permits Jeremiah to move on

past despair to buoyancy. Indeed, it is in the specific, concrete expression of despair that there come the seeds and possibilities of hope.... Consider the alternative. If Jeremiah had not spoken the despair in 8:18–9:3, it would not have been verbalized anguish but would have become immobilizing, unexpressed rage. It would have stricken him and blocked any possibility of hope. Thus, the despair of 8:18–9:3 is not the antithesis or denial of hope. It is an essential "door to hope."[14]

As with Jeremiah, so with us. And do not underestimate the power of *mere* words in these situations. There are words, lines, and paragraphs from crisis sermons that spoke to my pain so perfectly that I can remember them years later. On Moratorium Day in October 1968, in the midst of war and betrayal and uncertainty, Dr. James Sanders preached the greatest sermon I have ever heard, one he called "In the Same Night." And I learned of a certainty that in the very same night that we betrayed him, he broke bread and gave it to us, and that because even Judas was not excluded, I had a place at that table.[15]

I suppose the most famous series of crisis sermons ever preached was the Homilies on the Statues. The occasion was a serious civic upheaval in Antioch in February of the year 387 C.E. At that time the emperor Theodosius I had instituted a new tax upon the people. Consternation gave way to frenzy, and a riot broke out, which culminated in the statues of the emperor and his family being pulled down and dragged through the streets. Almost as soon as the riot was over, the anger over the tax was replaced by fear, since the insurrectionary acts were punishable by death. Many people were rounded up and executed. People barred themselves in their homes, and many fled to the mountains. The emperor threatened to destroy the entire city. Old Bishop Flavian left Antioch to go plead with the emperor in Constantinople for mercy. In his place a young, newly ordained presbyter gathered the people together and stood up to preach. His name was John. We call him Chrysostom. He began like this:

> What shall I say, or what shall I speak of? The present season is one for tears, and not for words; for lamentation, not for discourse; for prayer, not for preaching. Such is the magnitude of the deeds daringly done; so incurable is the wound, so deep the blow, even beyond the power of all treatment, and craving assistance from above.... Suffer me to mourn over our present state. Suffer me to open my mouth today and bewail this common calamity....
>
> Who, beloved, hath bewitched us? . . . Nothing was more dignified than our city! Now, never was anything more pitiable.... I mourn now and lament, not for the greatness of that wrath which is to be expected, but for the extravagance of the frenzy which has been manifested.... How, I pray, are we to bear the shame of all that has been done? I find the word of instruction broken off by lamentation; scarcely am I able to open my mouth, to part my lips, to move my tongue, to utter a syllable![16]

Somehow Chrysostom found a way to open his mouth, because he preached on for twenty-one days, until the emperor relented and the city was saved! I will have more to say about these sermons shortly. In the meantime, remember the need of people in sorrow for a landscape where they can place their pain. Providing this landscape is, I know, sometimes very difficult. In the face of great pain and sorrow, words often seem to fail us. We open our mouths, and nothing comes out. As John Donne said, "Language, thou art too narrow, and too weake to ease us now; great sorrow cannot speake." But God does temper the wind to the shorn lamb, shorn of wool or shorn of words. The last prayer I pray before entering the pulpit is to remind me of God's words to Moses, "Now go, and I will be with your mouth and teach you what you are to speak"

(Exodus 4:12). Lamentation need not be voiced in the rhetoric of the Second Sophistic to be effective. It only needs to be voiced in faith, hope, and love.

GOD'S WAGONS

My third suggestion is drawn from a story deep within the Hebrew Scriptures. In the book of Genesis we read how Joseph was sold into slavery by his brothers and how he rose to become the governor of all the land of Egypt. Later, a famine came upon the land of Canaan, and old Jacob sent his remaining sons twice to buy food in Egypt. On the second trip they experienced a reconciliation with Joseph, who sent his brothers back to bring their father and families to Egypt, where the best of the land would be theirs. The text tells us that, by Pharaoh's command, Joseph also sent Pharaoh's wagons for provision and transport.

Old Jacob, sitting by his tent, saw a cloud of dust approaching and said, "It is my sons." He rose to greet them and they hurried to him with the news: "Joseph is still alive! He is even ruler over all the land of Egypt" (45:26). The text says that Jacob's heart fainted, because he did not believe them. Would you? But then Jacob saw another cloud of dust, and soon the wagons of Pharaoh himself came rolling into camp. When he saw the wagons which Joseph had sent for him, his spirit revived, and he said (v. 27), "Enough! My son Joseph is still alive. I must go and see him before I die."

The testimony of the messengers in this case was not enough. Just as our testimony is sometimes less than convincing. But when Jacob saw Pharaoh's wagons, which could not be sent by order of anyone but Pharaoh himself, he knew that it was true. It was David Gregg who first pointed out to me that the sons had control over Joseph's coat, which they had used to deceive their father years before, but they did not have control over Pharaoh's wagons.[17] To see the wagons was, in Jacob's word, "enough." It was proof positive. The wagons could be believed. This raises the question: does God have wagons? Are there assurances that can be given to people in crisis that are compelling in and of themselves, apart from our own feeble witness? Yes.

Scripture is a wagon. I have seen the most radical of modern clerics, whose disdain for the Bible is palpable, go scurrying through the debris of their offices, trying to find a Bible, because they had to make a death call and had no idea of how to handle that assignment apart from the truth of scripture. The Old and New Testaments not only challenge us to build the kingdom, they provide us with rock solid evidence of the abiding concern of God for the least of these. Jesus frequently appealed to Scripture in his preaching, using images common to the Old Testament, like vineyards and wicked tenants, and sometimes taking figurative passages and expanding them, like the time he said we should forgive others seventy times seven, a play on Genesis 4. Jesus remembered that the people to whom he spoke were familiar with Scripture. This may be a more risky assumption for us, but many of our folk have at least a nodding acquaintance with Scripture and respond to it. Chapter 7 seeks to enumerate a number of biblical texts into which preachers and people may wish to climb during a variety of crises.

The Eucharist is also a wagon, a big wagon. Pharaoh's wagons proved absolutely to Jacob that there was someone in Egypt who loved him. The Lord's Supper proves absolutely that there is someone in heaven who loves us. When the old Park Avenue Christian Church in New York burned on a Sunday morning, the people huddled in tears on the pavement. Someone went across the street to a Jewish delicatessen and bought some matzoth and Manischewitz. There on the sidewalk, warmed by the smoldering ruins of the building, the living church broke bread and celebrated the abiding love of God. On the Moratorium Day of 1968 that I mentioned, when we were bewildered, not knowing which way to go, James Sanders had the vision to take us to the table.

We will shortly consider the crisis sermons preached by Martin Luther at Wittenburg in 1522. Suffice it to say here that the church at Wittenburg was falling apart. There was anger and hostility and fear. As I have written elsewhere:

> People were lost and confused. They did not know what to do or which way to go. Luther stood up and, in the midst of their suffering, offered them the Lord's Supper. He spoke to them about the peace a Christian could find in Communion, and he closed with these words: "For this bread is a comfort to the sorrowing, a healing for the sick, a life for the dying, a food for the hungry, and rich treasure for all the poor and needy."[18]

I wish I had said that, but I am glad that he did. For he has found us all in those few words, found us at our own level of weakness and pain. And for those of us who are sorrowing, sick, dying, hungry, poor and needy, he holds out the Eucharist as comfort, healing, life, food, and treasure. There is a blessing for every need here. How good it is to come to this table, even if just for a minute, to receive that peace of God which the world of its own accord cannot give.[19] Is there a better place to gather "when the world tumbles in" than the table of Jesus Christ? I know of none.

There are other wagons. The cross is a wagon, not one that says "God's in heaven; all's right with the world," but one that testifies that God saw the evil in the world and stayed through. What wondrous love that is! The empty tomb is a wagon. Are there four greater words in the New Testament than "He is not here?"

There is also something in an honest, faithful sermon that is a wagon as well. We may not understand all mysteries or be able to open the heavens to our people, but we can lay before them what Leonard Sweet calls the "great rocky facts of being," facts like: God loves us; God is not mocked; God had the first word, God had the second Word, and God will have the last word.[20] Ronald Osborn tells a story about Ivan Lee Holt, pastor of Saint John's Church in Saint Louis and a celebrated preacher, before he was made a bishop in the old Methodist Episcopal Church, South. One Sunday he looked out and to his delight saw his favorite professor from Chicago, the distinguished Old Testament scholar, J. M. Powis Smith. After church they greeted one another cordially and rejoiced in fond memories. Then Mrs. Smith drew the preacher aside to tell him that her husband had only recently learned that he had not long to live. He had borne the knowledge stoically. But that week he had said to his wife, "Let's go to Saint Louis for Sunday. I want to hear Holt preach one more time."[21]

I suggested in a previous chapter that crises need to be engaged theologically and that three of the greatest theological affirmations that can be made in crisis situations involve remembrance, presence, and promise. Here I reaffirm that and suggest that sometimes these assurances may best be carried to church in one of God's wagons. We "do this in remembrance of him" at the table. We recall God's presence in human form and God's unending, unutterable love for us when we confront "the old rugged cross." And we bear witness to the promise of God every time we recall the empty tomb or baptize a person into Christ: crucified, risen, and coming again. The point is that although crises must indeed be engaged theologically, to do so at a high level of abstraction may be counterproductive. In the fourth century, Saint Ambrose asserted: "the events under the Law were the *shadow*, the sacraments of the Gospel are the *image*, while perfect *truth* belongs to heaven where Christ already is and where one day we shall be."[22] Those of us who live between the shadow and the truth are desperate for those sacramental images of how it is going to be. So, when you find yourself and your people in crisis, drive God's wagons into the sanctuary, circle them around the people, and *show* them the shelter that the wagons can provide beneath the everlasting arms.

THE NEED FOR CONTINUITY

The fourth suggestion has to do with continuity. I have already addressed Chrysostom's Homilies on the Statues. Another impressive series of crisis sermons was preached in Wittenburg in 1522 by the great reformer himself, Martin Luther. Like Chrysostom, Luther preached each of these sermons not knowing with certainty whether he would be spared to preach the next one. Following the Diet of Worms, Luther had been hidden for his safety in the Wartburg Castle. Meanwhile, radicals had seized the reformation at Wittenburg and gone much further than Luther thought wise in eradicating all elements of the old system. At great peril, Luther went back to Wittenburg in March of 1522 and preached for eight straight days. These are among the most powerful sermons he ever preached. In them he told the people of their freedom in Christ, but he further admonished them not to make a "free" into a "must." The great iconoclast preached that although all things may be lawful, all things are not helpful. He pointed out that the work of reform required patience and humility. Do not, out of spite, he said, make a free into a must.

I enjoy reading the Wittenburg Sermons and the Homilies on the Statues for their brilliance and because they still preach, all these hundreds of years later, which is something I cannot say about a lot of sermons I heard just last year. In both series is a measure of continuity with the past. I am most amazed by Chrysostom. He named the crisis, led his people in lamenting it, set before them the steadfast love of God, and then went right ahead to preach on the text for the day! As his people stood before him, not knowing if they would live to see the morrow, he preached about such things as not swearing and not being a glutton at the dinner table. I thought to myself, "What is he doing? What do table manners have to do with survival?"

Then it hit me. Chrysostom and Luther knew something I did not: the crucial importance, especially in crisis, of continuity. One of the best ways to deal with the fear that tomorrow might not come is to prepare for tomorrow. One of the things that crises do to us is tear apart the order of our lives: "things fall apart; the centre cannot hold." As I once heard, "people can live without freedom for a long time, but they cannot live without order for a single day." Dictators know this, and use this human frailty to manipulate people. We need to know it as well to help people find their own order, their own reasons to get out of bed and face the day.

I do not want to be misunderstood here. I am not saying that we should fight change. We must all change or die. What I am saying is that in crisis, when all our structures of existence seem to have been ripped out from under us, we have a terrific need for a sense of continuity, for a feeling that somehow yesterday is connected to tomorrow. It was for the very reason that Chrysostom's people were not sure they would see tomorrow that he told them when tomorrow came, they were to watch their language and their diet. It was for the very reason that Luther's people were being stretched to the breaking point between what had been and what would be that he warned them not to throw out all the symbols and acts that had sustained them. For example, the radicals had thrown away the act of confession, about which Luther had this to say:

> Thus you see that confession must not be despised, but that it is a comforting thing. And since we need many absolu-

tions and assurances, because we must fight against the devil, death, hell, and sin, we must not allow any of our weapons to be taken away, but keep intact the whole armor and equipment which God has given us to use against our enemies. For you do not yet know what labor it costs to fight with the devil and overcome him. But I know it well, for I have eaten a bit of salt or two with him. I know him well, and he knows me well, too. If you had known him [as I know him], you would not have rejected confession in this way.[23]

Therefore do not be too hasty, for example, to discard the lectionary passages for the day. They may be just what you need. Do not even discard your sermon too hastily. Look at it to see if there is a text, a theme, that can be used to affirm Fiddler's words in *Roots* as he bent over the whipped and beaten Kunta Kinté, "There's gonna come another day; there's gonna come another day."[24]

Let me summarize: when the time of crisis comes and you climb into the pulpit, seek to name the crisis, the real crisis, and not just the present manifestation of it. If appropriate, express the lamentation of the people of God. Then set before your people the great eternal truths of the faith, the truths that have led us safe this far, and will, by the grace of God, lead us home.

A CALL FOR COURAGE

The week-in, week-out preaching of the gospel tests our discipline and creativity. Preaching the gospel in crisis tests our mettle. Therefore I say, in epilogue to the other suggestions, crisis preaching calls for courage. The good news in crisis may be bad news to some, and the gospel faithfully preached may not be popular.[25] So gird up your loins, and take heart. Those who have preached faithfully before you and those who will come after are depending upon you in this moment. One of the first preachers in the New World was a friar named Antonio de Montesinos. Shortly after New Spain was founded by those whose desire was to serve God and get rich, the greed of the Spaniards led the colony into crisis. On the fourth Sunday of Advent in 1511, Friar Antonio stood up and preached a sermon entitled "The Rock Hard Wilderness of the Spanish Heart." The reaction was swift and harsh. Montesinos was summoned to a meeting with the governor and the father superior. He was instructed to preach again the next Sunday and retract what he had said. When Friar Antonio mounted the pulpit the next Sunday, everybody who was anybody in New Spain was there. He began his sermon with these words, "That which I have already said, I say again . . . ," and he proceeded to let them have it with the other barrel. This is the last we ever hear of Friar Antonio de Montesinos. But there was a young man in the congregation who was so moved by the sermon that he dedicated himself to the service of the oppressed and exploited Indians. Bartolomé de las Casas became a defender of the Indians, a great bishop and preacher, and author of *The Tears of the Indians*. He established early in the New World that preaching could and would be a force against imperialism.[26] Antonio de Montesinos. Bartolomé de las Casas. How could we let such preachers down when our time of crisis comes?

Two millennia of Christian preachers with courage have turned uprooted, devastated lives into new seedbeds for the gospel. To this day the seeds of the gospel will take root and grow when we faithfully execute the office to which we have been called. Therefore, my brothers and sisters, in season and out of season, when things are good and when things are bad, whether the sun shines or darkness covers the face of the earth, let us stand in the pulpit with courage, as preachers called by God to witness unto the truth and speak a good word for Jesus Christ, to whom be glory forever and ever.

CHAPTER SIX

THE STRUCTURE OF THE CRISIS SERMON

s there a particular form or structure that is best for crisis sermons? No. What Paul Scott Wilson says about sermons in general also applies to crisis preaching: "categories of overall form are of limited value."[1] Few good sermons are strictly propositional or narrative in form, since a unity imposed on material by a predetermined structure or genre is a *static* unity.[2] Good form is not predetermined then; it emerges in the hermeneutical process as gospel engages situation.

For example, we have considered the psychology of the crisis experience and pointed out the (somewhat tenuous) relationship between crisis counseling and preaching. Can, then, the methods used in crisis counseling be transferred to the pulpit? Not directly. Consider the method advocated by Stone and others: "The A-B-C method of pastoral crisis intervention has three elements: (A) *A*chieve contact with the person; (B) *B*oil down the problem to its essentials; and (C) *C*ope actively with the problem."[3] Let us look at each of these through homiletical lenses.

Under (A), *achieving contact,* there are also important guides for preaching. Communication is enhanced when a relationship of trust exists. Such items as the importance of posture and eye contact by the caregiver apply to preaching as well. But most of Stone's emphasis on the establishment of an empathetic relationship focuses on listening to one person or a very small group. The preacher must listen as well, before he or she stands to speak: listen to the people, the experts, the text, the Spirit. However, in crisis, there may be precious little time to listen, to sort things out, before we are called upon to preach. Listening to all the voices we would like to hear is often impossible. Furthermore, we counsel individuals, but we preach to groups, groups composed of persons who respond to crises in different ways. So I fall back to what has already been said: If we have not already achieved contact (trust may be a better word here) with our people (through faithful ministry and personal attention), there is rarely time to do so in crisis.

Here are two examples of what I mean. I once heard a story about the great preacher Ernest Fremont Tittle.[4] Long-time pastor (1918–49) of the First Methodist Church in Evanston, Illinois, Tittle was an outspoken advocate for racial justice before that was a popular stance. Once, while he was out of town, the church elders gathered and several proposed that Tittle be fired. One elder, who had not yet spoken, then reminded them of his own experience with the pastor. A few years before, he and his wife had been sitting at home late one night when his wife slumped over in her chair. When the man became aware of this, he went over to her, but she was dead! He was stunned beyond belief. Things shortly got very hectic, with the arrival of medical personnel, police, neighbors, and others. The man was overwhelmed and suddenly burst from the house just as Tittle, who had been called, was coming up the walk. The man ran by Tittle and started down the street. Tittle turned and followed him. He fell into step with the man, about twenty paces behind, and followed him in this way all night long! Toward dawn, the man walked out onto a pier on Lake Michigan. He stopped at the end of the pier and looked down into the cold dark water. Tittle quietly walked up beside him, put his hand on his shoulder, called him by name, and said, "Would you like to go home now?" The man finished his story and then said that, although he did not always agree with Tittle's positions on the issues of the day, Tittle had won his trust and gratitude, and he would have nothing to do with this plan to fire him. Nothing more was—or could be—said, and the meeting was adjourned. That was contact achieved! The right to be heard had been earned.

On the other hand, consider this story from James Michener's *Centennial* about a young minister who visits a town in Colorado to preach his trial sermon:

'My text stands close to the heart of every true Christian, for better than any other it epitomizes the spirit of our Lord. It comes, fittingly, from the last chapter of the last Gospel, John 21.'

A rancher in the front pew who knew his Bible muttered, 'Oh, no!' but Reverend Bluntworthy in his firm, clear voice lined out the message: ' "Jesus saith to Simon Peter ... Feed my lambs.' " A whisper passed along the pews. ' "He saith to him a second time ... Feed my sheep.' " [People] looked at each other in confusion. ' "He saith unto him a third time, Simon, son of Jonas ... Feed my sheep.' "

From this unfortunate beginning Bluntworthy launched into a perfervid oration about sheep as the symbol of humankind, Jesus as the shepherd, and the world as a great meadow in which right-thinking men took it upon themselves as a holy obligation to *Feed my sheep.* He must have used this exhortation fifteen times, until at the end of his sermon he implored every man in the church to go forth and become a shepherd.[5]

The angry crowd tromped out by the side door, so they would not have to shake the hand of the miscreant. The would-be preacher knew not what he had done until his host finally said to him, "The Lord may be partial to sheep, but this is Hereford country."[6] The preacher did not know to whom he was preaching, and his sermon consequently was not heard. No contact was achieved although a valuable lesson was surely learned.

The lesson learned in both instances was that there is no substitute for the daily, weekly pastoral relationship that builds up a reservoir of trust and respect that can be drawn upon in crisis. I recommend, then, that when one is new in a congregation or has a group in crisis that one does not know well or whose trust has not yet been earned, it is best to lean on the one who *has* earned their trust and the right to speak: Jesus Christ. This is especially true in funerals. All ministers from time to time are called upon to preach at the funerals of people they did not know. I have often heard some form of the following phrase used: "Although I did not have the privilege of knowing Mrs. Jones, I am sure that she was a fine person." There is no contact and little succor in that kind of language. It is better to find out what the family wants remembered about her and then say something like this: "Family and friends remember Eula Jones as one who cared for her family, her home and garden, her church and community. Jesus remembers her that way, too, and will care for her forever."

(B) *Boiling down* the crisis to its essentials is important to the sermon as well, as we have seen in the section on *Naming the Monster.* However, many homileticians have a negative reaction to the "boiling down" process. Craddock points out the problem when he says, "Much preaching that aims at propositions and themes and outlines does just that: the minister boils off all the water and preaches the stain in the bottom of the cup."[7] He once illustrated this by saying, "It's like a father who goes in to his children at bedtime, all tucked in with their flannel pajamas and camphor cloth, and says, 'Kids, I don't have time for the story tonight, but the point of the story is this....'"[8] Another way of stating the problem is to say that the boiling down process often reduces the experience of the crisis to an abstract concept. And people in crisis may be unable to deal with too much abstraction, overwhelmed as they are by powerful memories and a flood of emotion. The statement "Our basic problem today is one of ontology" may in fact be true, but it may neither be helpful nor heard. Focus on the essentials in crisis, yes; but do not boil all the imagery and tension and hope out of the message.

Finally, Stone suggests (C) *Coping actively with the problem.* Yes, but. Coping never resolves anything. Coping suggests, rather, that we find ways to live with (or within) the crisis. There may be times when that is all we can do. But it is not finally the way of the gospel. "Learning to live with your sin" is not a particularly hopeful sermon topic. Instead of coping, the gospel is finally about resurrection. There is a difference. The Gerasene demoniac in Luke 8 had learned to cope with his demons, had accepted that his name was "Legion." But Jesus told the demons to leave. We will discuss shortly how people are more open to change in times of crisis than times of stasis. There are occasions when such moments must be seized.

The point of the past few paragraphs is not to denigrate the A-B-C model of crisis intervention, but to suggest that it does not translate to preaching without careful reflection. Returning now to the matter of form: since the situation is a factor in creating form, and we are speaking of crisis situations, there is one suggestion about form too obvious to be ignored. And for those who appreciate models, the suggestion leads us toward one.

Stone uses Morley's diagram of a crisis to demonstrate a person's "heightened psychological accessibility," which is one way of saying that people in crisis are open to change.[9]

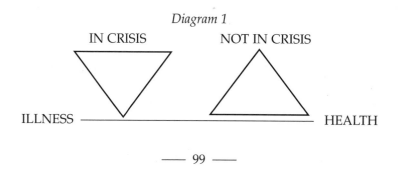

Diagram 1

IN CRISIS   NOT IN CRISIS

ILLNESS ———————————————— HEALTH

As the diagram shows, persons not in crisis are relatively stable. One side of the triangle rests on the line between health and illness. In crisis, however, the triangle sits on one of its points. It, and the person it represents, are much less stable. They can easily fall (or be pushed) in one direction or the other. Stone says:

> During the period of crisis, with individuals' greater susceptibility to change, less counseling is required to aid them toward effective resolution of their problems. The difficulty frequently is that we do not help soon enough. When the crisis stage is past, it takes more leverage to bring change because the "triangle" is back on its base. The brief period when the triangle is tipped up is so significant because of the emotional intensity, the cognitive dissonance, the loosened boundaries, and the heightened vulnerability. Successful crisis intervention makes maximum use of the heightened psychological accessibility of individuals and families [and congregations?] in crisis. All crisis counseling is based upon this principle.[10]

Consider this important statement homiletically. It reinforces what we have already said about the importance of engaging crises homiletically, rather than ignoring them until later when we and the people have stabilized. There is a window to growth in crisis situations that may be closed at other times. The downside to this for preaching is threefold: (1) since people in crisis may not process information rationally, they may mishear or not hear an abstract message; (2) they may be especially vulnerable to manipulative sermons; and, of course, (3) creating good sermons in a very brief time is extremely difficult.

By way of analogy, compare my use of Morley's diagram with the following adaptation of Locke Bowman's diagram of teaching (and preaching) styles from Fred Craddock's *As One Without Authority* [11]:

Diagram 2

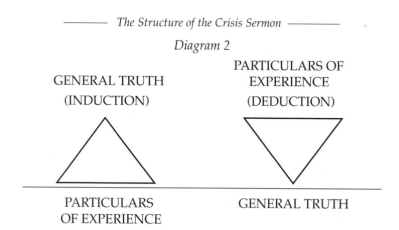

GENERAL TRUTH
(INDUCTION)

PARTICULARS OF
EXPERIENCE
(DEDUCTION)

PARTICULARS
OF EXPERIENCE

GENERAL TRUTH

The deductive sermon begins with an affirmation and moves toward application. It sits (and often teeters) on its *point*, and if that point, especially when abstracted, cannot be processed by hearers, then the triangle (and the sermon) tips over and falls. In contrast, the inductive sermon sits on the particulars of experience and then moves toward the affirmation of a general truth. In my experience it is better, whether one uses the language of induction versus deduction or not,[12] to begin a crisis sermon with the "particulars of experience." We begin with the acknowledgment of what has happened to us and our world. Journalist Katie Sherrod calls this "speaking the truth that is in the room."[13] She also calls it essential in dealing with a crisis. In one sermon that I have seen, preached three days after a tornado had cut a terrible swath right through town, the preacher moved in the first paragraph to a discussion of God's will, using Weatherhead's classic analysis. The preacher's goal was laudable, but what he did, in effect, was to deny the truth that was in the room: that some of the people were injured and homeless; that everyone was stunned, cut loose from the moorings of things as they were, and adrift on a sea of confusion and grief. These were feelings that somehow needed to be verbalized or imaged (*creatively lamented* as it were) before abstract theological concepts could be processed.

With reference to the triangles, Craddock also suggests that they can be, and often are, stacked in a sermon. Ronald Allen puts it this way:

> In the overall pattern of arrangement, a preacher may spend the first ten minutes in inductive development—raising an issue, analyzing it theologically, and coming to a conclusion. In the second ten minutes, the preacher may use the major conclusion as a premise that is applied deductively to the situation of the listeners. This results in a sermon that can be diagrammed as an hourglass.[14]

Diagram 3

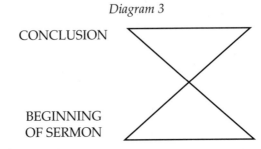

CONCLUSION

BEGINNING
OF SERMON

This is much more helpful. The preacher does boil down the viscous crisis, come to a point, "name the monster," and proclaim the gospel. I am tempted to leave it at that. However, we must recall that Allen's is a model set forth for ordinary time and not crisis. The "squeeze" has been moved, but the model is still unstable. And there are crisis sermons that cannot be reduced to one point or one affirmation.

Here I risk swimming against the tide of contemporary homiletics, which is deeply vested in the one-clear-thought, sermon-in-a-sentence approach to preaching, by going back over 150 years to the method of the English preacher, Frederick W. Robertson. Robertson advocated the two-point or bipolar sermon. He searched for truth in the dialectic or polar structures of the text and situation, saying that "the truth is made up of two opposite propositions, and not found in a *via media* between the two."[15] In crisis preaching, we might see the "two opposite propositions" to which Robertson refers as the bad news of our situation and the good news of the gospel. Neither can be ignored. Nor are we looking for a *via media*. We are searching in the tension between the two for a glimpse of God's promised outcome and the way for us to get there. Take life and death. Neither can exist without the other. But there is real tension between the two, a tension we are not trying to cope with or finesse or smooth over. That would result in a living death. We are in quest of the promise that death shall be swallowed up in victory. It may be better, then, to envision the sermon in crisis in the following way:

Diagram 4

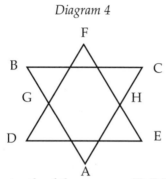

In this view the truth of the sermon (D,E,F) is laid over the truth of the situation (A,B,C) in such a way that some stabilizing support is offered, the tension in the situation is engaged, and the gospel is proclaimed. It begins with the particulars of experience, seeking to speak the truth that is in the room. This acknowledging of the crisis is painted in broad enough strokes that most of the points various people may be standing (or teetering) upon—pain, anger, guilt— are included. The sermon thus provides a landscape which, although it does not stop the pain, may help to contain it. The sermon then moves through engagement with the tension between situation and gospel to an affirmation of the good news in the midst of our crisis. Suggestions may then also be offered as to how the good news may be experienced and applied. The design is such that, just as the particular pain of the individual or group is contained in the opening acknowledgment of crisis, the message of hope is contained within the closing section, where the consequences of faith are proclaimed. Thus, although the overall shape of the sermon resembles a *mogen David*,[16] each person "hears" a diamond (A,G,F,H). That is to say, their particular concerns—one or many—are acknowledged (A), the tension between situation and gospel is engaged (G,H), and a direction is suggested (F). Because the preacher is fallible and has perhaps been immobilized by the crisis just like his or her people, the message may be a very rough-cut diamond, to be sure, with fewer facets or windows to hope than we would like. But it may reflect just the light that people need in order to see their way through. For that we give thanks.

One should not make too much of any diagram purporting to cover every situation. Again, no single form is normative. All I am trying to suggest with this model is that, unlike propositional or deductive sermons, which simply mirror the person(s) in crisis (both perhaps resting on a shaky point), or the hourglass sermon, which narrows to such a point, it is better to use a form that takes the crisis into account and provides a broad enough base to help support the people in their unsettling experience. At no place in the model that I propose are the persons in crisis left without support. The "heard sermon," represented by the diamond, acknowledges the crisis in which we find ourselves, proclaims the gospel over against the evil and suffering, and proposes a direction we may take from here. It does all of this in a supportive way in the midst of a supportive community.

Let me anticipate a critique. It might be argued that the model is, frankly, too broad or, worse, too wishy-washy. One cannot preach to all crisis responses at once (confusion, guilt, fear, and so forth); nor can one suggest enough gospel trajectories to meet every need. To do so is to end up with a mishmash of slogans instead of a sermon. This could happen. I know. I have seen it. I have probably done it more often than I would care to admit. But when it happens, it tends to be a failure of courage and imagination rather than a failure of the model. Trying to cover all the crisis responses in the congregation does not mean spending five minutes or even one minute on each one. It means acknowledging them. "Some of us have feelings of grief this morning; others of us are angry." Nor does it relieve us of the effort to name the *real* monster in our midst. "Given all the feelings about the bombing that we bring with us to church this morning, let's focus for a few minutes on two of them, the powerful sense of anger and our desperate desire for revenge."

In conclusion, what does this mean in the real world of (rushed) sermon preparation? In the midst of a significant crisis, people are struggling with a variety of feelings and questions. They cannot all be dealt with (at least helpfully) in a sermon. But many of them can be acknowledged. The gospel can then be brought to bear on the situation. And, finally, the various consequences of that engagement can be pointed out in a supportive, compelling way. The sermon, while engaging the crisis, stands over against it with a word from God. While preachers have never had, and do not now have, the luxury (or burden) of an A-B-C approach to preaching—and while no single form is the best for all situations—I affirm that a sermon which begins by acknowledging the crisis[17] and then moves to God's hopeful word for us[18] has a better chance of being heard and being helpful.

Here is an excerpt from a recent sermon based on Job 42 that effectively portrays the crisis in which both Job and a modern woman found themselves. The preacher is laying the groundwork for an affirmation of faith:

Last fall I was at the State Fair looking at the Creative Arts exhibits. There was everything from jars of ruby plum jelly and emerald green sweet pickles to photographs of lush bluebonnets and portraits of quaint Southern Belles. Everything displayed there had an air of pride and perfection about it. Well, almost everything. Along the wall where the quilts were displayed for everyone to marvel at their intricate stitching and careful patchwork, there was a sort of tapestry—a quilted tapestry—about one foot by two feet in size. Something about it didn't seem right. First, it appeared rather unremarkable there among all the other fluffy and frilly quilts. It was white with six blue gingham stars arranged in pairs along its length. The first was a perfect seven-point star, but each successive star was missing a point, until the final star had only two points. The typed index card next to it explained the odd arrangement. The tapestry's creator had made it in memory of her mother, who was in the advanced stages of Alzheimers's disease. The stars represented the progression of the disease and the gradual toll it had taken from its victim and her loved ones. I could only imagine the pain that each frame of that tapestry represented as its star diminished, point by point.

I wonder how long it took the creator of that touching tapestry to find such an expression of her sense of loss. She, like Job, had discovered a way to depict the unexplainable, a way to deal with her grief. She had created from scraps and thread an expression of reality and truth. She had shared the blessings of her discovery with all who stood to look at her creation. From the scraps of his own life Job has stitched his own tapestry, re-sewing the fabric of his being with the thread of faith. He repairs his friendship with Eliphaz, Bildad, and Zophar with the thread of prayer. The result is for all to see, to understand a new and more profound purpose in the presence of a loving and faithful God. This is the understanding that brings blessings from despair and hope from darkness. See, and proclaim a blessing.[19]

See the situation. See the gospel. See the sermon.

CHAPTER SEVEN

BIBLICAL RESOURCES FOR CRISIS SERMONS: AN ANNOTATED LECTIONARY

*T*his chapter is offered with some anxiety. A case can be made that any biblical text is appropriate for any situation. I have heard enough preachers say that the lectionary text for the day proved to be just what they needed that I cannot dismiss their claims as mere serendipity. I have also just finished saying in the previous chapter that continuity is important in crisis situations and that preachers should not discard too quickly the texts they have planned to use. Nevertheless, we cannot escape two facts about crisis sermons: (1) although all texts may be appropriate, some may be more helpful, vivid, and compelling than others for particular situations, and (2) in many crises there is very little time to conduct a search for the best, most useful word.

This chapter, then, is offered to suggest helpful texts for specific kinds of crises, along with a possible approach to that text in a sermon. This is not to say that there may not be other, more useful texts to consider. The Bible, from beginning to end, is a sort of crisis literature, filled with tensions. In Genesis 1 there is too much water; in Genesis 2 there is not enough. Until God acts. The last two gifts of God mentioned in Revelation 22 are water for the thirsty and plagues for the blasphemers. All is contingent on God's grace. The preacher knows the exigencies of his or her situation, and just the right text may leap to mind. But sometimes crises erode or numb our minds' leaping ability, and some suggestions may be appreciated. A further note: we cannot always look for one-to-one correspondences between text and situation. Nor should we. There are no plane crashes in the Bible. But there are occasions of great tragedy and loss of life and clues about responding in faith.

At least one text from both the Hebrew Bible and the New Testament, along with a reading from the Psalter, is offered for the various named crises. A word about the use of psalms in preaching may be helpful. As Emilie Townes said in a lecture on the poetics of crisis, "synchronic experience cannot be reduced to linear language."[1] Psalm texts, then, with their rhythmic, often nonlinear language, may be particularly appropriate and useful when preaching in crisis. Unfortunately, compilers of the Revised Common Lectionary did not intend the listed psalms to be readings and grist for preaching but rather responses to other texts.[2] This follows a long-standing, and to my mind bad, tradition of using the psalms as secondary rather than primary theological material, material to be sung or recited but not critically engaged. And on those rare occasions when preachers do use a psalm as a text for a sermon, many tend to use it as they would prosaic texts. When one ignores the form of a text, extracts some point, and then crafts a sermon in a form completely different from that of the text, the text is violated and its ability to speak through its form as well as its content is lost. While it is relatively easy to "extract a point and ignore the form" with prose texts, it is more difficult with poetry. It is hard to imagine the psalms without their poetic language and rhythm. Sermons that do so also tend to be flat and lifeless. Psalms are poetic liturgical prayers. As Thomas Long says, they "operate at the level of the imagination, often swiveling the universe on the hinges of a single image."[3] A sermon based on a psalm need not be a poem (though it might be), but it does need to pay attention to the evocative language and rhythm and imagery of the text.

I. PUBLIC CRISES

A. Natural Disasters

In the known universe, God has provided a very small space in which we can live. Too hot or too cold, too much light or not enough, too much water or not enough, too much air pressure or not enough ... and we die. We take the natural world for granted, as if it were here for our pleasure alone. When this natural world slips its normal boundaries and goes wild, our lives also bounce from normalcy into crisis. We are, as the song says, like "sparrows in a hurricane,"[4] unable to stand or understand. We are desperate for a word of comfort.

1. Wind and Water:
Storms, Tornadoes, Hurricanes, Floods, Avalanches

a. Isaiah 54:9-4

> *O afflicted one, storm-tossed, and not comforted,*
> *I am about to set your stones in antimony,*
> *and lay your foundations with sapphires.*

This text offers three promises of God in the face of such peril:

1. God will no longer punish humanity by storm (9*a*).
2. God is not about the business of punishment (9*b*).
3. Despite the suffering brought about through forces of nature, nothing can separate us from the love of God (10-11). Amen.

b. Job 38:29-30

> *From whose womb did the ice come forth,*
> *and who has given birth to the hoarfrost of heaven?*

The voice from the whirlwind pelts Job with questions that he cannot answer. This is one of them. Ice and snow are lovely, but like Job, we do not understand them, especially when they turn against us and cause suffering and death. Job stands mute in the face of the relentless questioning until chapter 42, when he finally realizes that, in spite of everything, God's purposes will not be thwarted. Job, and we, may not have been blessed with understanding, but we have been blessed by the presence of God.

c. Acts 27:13-44

We were being pounded by the storm.... Paul then stood up among them and said...: "Keep up your courage, men, for I have faith in God."

Providence in the face of peril. A good text in the face of an impending storm, like a hurricane or blizzard. The sailors panicked; Paul reacted with the calmness of one with insight into the future. Work, as the sailors did, yes. But like Paul, pray. Keep focus on God and row for shore.

d. Psalm 93

The floods have lifted up, O LORD, ...
The floods lift up their roaring.
More majestic than the thunders of mighty waters, ...
majestic on high is the Lord!

This is a simple, powerful affirmation of faith. No matter how overwhelming the flood waters appear, we affirm that the majesty of God is great still and there place our trust.

e. Psalm 107:23-32

Then they cried to the LORD in their trouble,
and he brought them out from their distress;
he made the storm be still....

The experience of a storm as a people of God:
1. Normal, everyday living (23-24).

2. The storm comes, and the people experience the emotional roller coaster of riding out the storm (25-27).

3. Faith issues: crying out to the Lord; prayer for help, peace, understanding; God's awesome power; new appreciation for the quiet that follows; sense of gratitude (28-31).

4. What we are doing now, gathered as we are in worship (32).

Other texts: Genesis 7, Isaiah 30:20, Jonah 1–2, Matthew 7:24-27, Mark 4:35-41, and Revelation 12:15.

2. Lack of Water: Drought

a. Deuteronomy 32:1-13

> *Give ear, O heavens, and I will speak; . . .*
> *May my teaching drop like the rain,*
> *my speech condense like the dew;*
> *like gentle rain on grass, like showers on new growth.*

When the land is dry and parched, nothing brings relief like a gentle, steady rain. When the soul is dry as dust, nothing is more comforting than the Word of God.

b. Jeremiah 14:1-9

> *Judah mourns and her gates languish. . . . Her nobles send their servants for water; they come to the cisterns, they find no water, they return with their vessels empty. . . . Because there has been no rain in the land the farmers are dismayed; they cover their heads.*

Jeremiah's touching lament during a drought captures feelings we have to this day. Why should we be ashamed, like those in Jeremiah's lament? Because without water, we cannot farm, we cannot grow, we cannot clean, we cannot be human beings. And that frustrates and shames us. Jeremiah then does a most interesting thing. He does not call on God to end the drought; he calls on God not to abandon the people: "Yet you, O LORD, are in the midst of us, and we are called by your name; do not forsake us!" Our identity lies not in what we do or what the earth does. We are called by God's name, and there only do we have life.

c. John 4:7-15

> *"Everyone who drinks of this water will be thirsty again,*
> *but those who drink of the water that*
> *I will give them will never be thirsty.*
> *The water that I will give will become in them*
> *a spring of water*
> *gushing up to eternal life."*

A reminder that, as we pray for water upon the dry land, we also need to pray for the living water of God, the water that quenches thirst forever and leads to eternal life.

d. Psalm 63:1-4

> *O God, you are my God, I seek you,*
> *my soul thirsts for you;*
> *my flesh faints for you,*
> *as in a dry and weary land where there is no water.*

The Bible often uses drought imagery to describe desiccated human spirits. God's love is pictured as moisture upon the land. Be faithful during the dry times of trial, and do not forget who sustained you when, at last, the drought is over.

Other texts: Genesis 2:4-7, Amos 4:6-8, 1 Kings 18:41-46, Matthew 4:1-11, Jude 11–13, and Revelation 22:1-3.

3. Earthquake

a. Zechariah 14:1-6

> *. . . you shall flee as you fled from the earthquake*
> *in the days of King Uzziah of Judah.*
> *Then the LORD my God will come,*
> *and all the holy ones with him.*

Both Amos (1:1) and Zechariah (14:5) refer to an earthquake during the reign of King Uzziah. Earthquakes are such devastating events that time is marked by them. People feel helpless and numbed before power of that magnitude. But even if it seems that God is not in the earthquake (1 Kings 19:11), scripture reminds us that God is never far, that God will come to us and bring comfort.

b. Matthew 28:1-10

> *After the sabbath, as the first day of the week was dawning,*
> *Mary Magdalene and the other Mary went to see the tomb.*
> *And suddenly there was a great earthquake;*
> *for an angel of the Lord, descending from heaven,*
> *came and rolled back the stone and sat on it.*

The power of God is so awesome that its manifestation is often pictured as accompanied by great natural events, like earthquakes. Perhaps, recovering from an earthquake that has shattered their lives, people can, in time, hear about the gospel earthquake, which heralded the resurrection of Christ and made all things new. As we struggle to stand up from this disaster, let us ask God to not make us the way we were before, but new people in Christ.

c. Psalm 18:1-19

> *Then the earth reeled and rocked;*
> *the foundations also of the mountains trembled*
> *and quaked, because he was angry. . . .*
> *but the* LORD *was my support.*
> *He brought me out into a broad place;*
> *he delivered me, because he delighted in me.*

Earthquakes not only manifest God's power in scripture, but also God's anger, anger at those who oppress the people of God. Natural disasters do not discriminate between rich and poor, but the aftermath does. The Psalmist's cry is for justice; the Psalmist's plea is for compassion.

Other texts: Exodus 19:16-25, Psalm 68:7-10, Luke 21:10-19, Acts 16:25-4, and Revelation 11:12-14, Psalm 68:7-10.

4. Fire

a. Exodus 3:1-6
> *He looked, and the bush was blazing,*
> *yet it was not consumed.*

That which is of God cannot be consumed by fire. This was one of the lessons Moses learned when he stood before the burning-yet-not-consumed bush and experienced one of the central theophanies in the history of our faith. The bush burned, but God's presence was not consumed. Our church building has burned, but the church has not been consumed.

b. Daniel 3
> *"If it be so, our God whom we serve is able*
> *to deliver us from the burning fiery furnace,*
> *and he will deliver us out of thine hand, O king.*
> *But if not, be it known unto thee, O king,*
> *that we will not serve thy gods*
> *nor worship the golden image which thou hast set up." (KJV)*

The story of Shadrach, Meshach, and Abednego, cast into the fiery furnace by Nebuchadnezzar, has moved people for millennia. Two thoughts from it today: (1) After the three were thrown into the fire, the king was amazed and asked his counselors, "Was it not three men that we threw bound into the fire?" Assured that they had, the king said, "But I see four men unbound, walking in the middle of the fire, and they are not hurt; and the fourth has the appearance of a god." The three were not alone in their ordeal by fire, neither are we. (2) And although they were delivered, remember their promise that, even should they not be spared from suffering, they would not abandon their faith. We pray for deliverance as well. But even if we are not spared, we also will not abandon our faith.

c. Matthew 3:1-12

> *"I baptize you with water for repentance,*
> *but one who is more powerful than I*
> *is coming after me; I am not worthy to carry his sandals.*
> *He will baptize you with the Holy Spirit and fire."*

Baptism by fire has entered our vocabulary to describe a particularly difficult ordeal. We remember how Jesus was baptized by John in the Jordan and then went into the wilderness for his *real* baptism. Sometimes we, who have been baptized by water, must also endure the baptism by fire. As we endure the second, let us not forget the first. We have died unto the world and been claimed by Christ. We are his, and no destruction or temptation can change that.

d. Psalm 74:1-8

> *They set your sanctuary on fire;*
> *they desecrated the dwelling place of your name,*
> *bringing it down to the ground....*
> *They burned all the meeting places of God in the land....*
> *How long, O God, is the foe to scoff?*

People may feel helpless and hopeless after great loss by fire, and they may need to give voice to their lamentation. This psalm helps us to do so. We may then follow with the affirmations offered in the three preceding texts.

Other texts: Zechariah 11:1-3, Wisdom of Solomon 3, 1 Corinthians 3:10-15, and Hebrews 12:25-29.

B. Other Disasters

The suddenness of many tragedies is stunning. There is an Enoch-like quality to them: "Enoch walked with God; and he *was* not" (Genesis 5:24 KJV). Gone. In the twinkling of an eye. Our friends and loved ones were there a few minutes ago, and now they are not. There is no time to prepare, to marshal our forces. We are cast into a maelstrom of grief and confusion. We need a lifeline. We need God.

1. Explosions; Crashes; Collapse of Buildings, Dams, and Bridges

a. Job 9:22-23

> *[God] destroys both the blameless and the wicked.*
> *When disaster brings sudden death, he mocks*
> *at the calamity of the innocent.*

Job is the great investigation of theodicy in the Bible. The main question of the book is, Why? Finally, of course, there is no answer, only the recognition of our finitude and God's majesty. But there is good news. God, who does not have to do so, cares. This text from early in the book shows Job's lament that God seems not to care and even mocks when disaster falls upon the innocent. It took Job a long time to learn that he was wrong. When the sparrow falls, when people suffer, God is present and God cares.

b. 1 Thessalonians 5:1-11

> *When they say, "There is peace and security," then sudden destruction*
> *will come upon them, as labor pains come upon a pregnant woman, and*
> *there will be no escape! ... But ... God has destined us not for wrath*
> *but for obtaining salvation through our Lord Jesus Christ, who died for*
> *us, so that whether we are awake or asleep we might live with him.*

There is no better place in scripture to see a Christian response to disaster than in this text. Responding to questions about the Day of the Lord, Paul uses similes and metaphors relating that day to other difficult days the people may have experienced. It will come "like a thief in the night." The destruction will come "as labor pains come upon a pregnant woman." The destruction will be sudden, massive, and unexpected—like some things we also have known. But, Paul reminds them and us, God has not destined us for wrath but for salvation, whether we live now or die. Therefore encourage and build up one another, that in faith, love, and hope we may endure unto salvation.

c. Psalm 34

> *When the righteous cry for help, the LORD hears,*
> *and rescues them from all their troubles.*
> *The LORD is near to the brokenhearted,*
> *and saves the crushed in spirit.*

The Psalmist gives personal witness to God having saved him from all his troubles, and he encourages his listeners to have the same faith. Unexpected disasters, especially those that result in loss of life, are different from slow terminal illnesses. We are left benumbed, uncomprehending, without even having been able to say good-bye. This psalm affirms two critical things in those situations: God is near; God saves.

Other texts: Joshua 6:15-21, Job 1:13-22, Psalm 77, Luke 13:1-5, and Acts 27:39-44.

2. Disease and Epidemics

a. 2 Kings 5

> *So he went down and immersed himself seven times*
> *in the Jordan, according to the word of the man of God;*
> *his flesh was restored like the flesh of a young boy, and he was clean.*

Few things strike fear into the heart of people like epidemics. Fourteenth-century Europe was decimated by plague. Nineteenth-century American towns were wiped out in a single day by cholera. Outbreaks of influenza killed hundreds of thousands in early twentieth-century America. More recently, there was polio. The current menace is AIDS.

Hardly helpful are texts such as Numbers 25, in which epidemic is tied to sin and the cure is found in ritual murder. More helpful is the marvelous story of Naaman and Elisha in 2 Kings 5, in which Naaman the leper learns that healing power rests not in "*some* great thing" (KJV) but in the word of God. Today's doctors are coming to accept the importance of spiritual activity in the healing process. God heals. We can help, all of us, whether through skilled medical practice or prayer or presence.

b. Mark 2:1-12
> "*Which is easier, to say to the paralytic, 'Your sins are forgiven,'*
> *or to say, 'Stand up and take your mat and walk'?"*

Further evidence of the interrelation of spiritual and physical healing is found in the story of Jesus healing the paralytic. The scribes criticized Jesus, and his response joined spiritual healing ("your sins are forgiven") to physical healing ("stand up and take your mat and walk"). When faced with a situation in which it appears that "all we can do is pray," do not underestimate the power of that action.

c. Psalm 51:10-12
> *Create in me a clean heart, O God,*
> *and put a new and right spirit within me.*
> *Do not cast me away from your presence,*
> *and do not take your holy spirit from me.*
> *Restore me to the joy of your salvation,*
> *and sustain in me a willing spirit.*

While God's healing power is a great gift, mightier still is the blessing of God's presence. Illness and even death can be endured in the shelter of the Most High. We pray for healing, yes, but even more fervently do we pray for the presence of God in the midst of our suffering.

Other texts: 1 Samuel 5–6; Psalms 6, 22, 38, 102; Matthew 8:14-17; and Luke 8:43-48.

C. Political Crises

1. Terrorism, War, and Rumors of War

Preaching about war and war-making is a difficult challenge. But it is one which wiser preachers than we have faced. See the bibliography for ideas from preachers who have struggled with this issue in the past.

a. Jeremiah 8:14-22

> *We look for peace, but find no good,*
> *for a time of healing, but there is terror instead.*

Terrorism as we understand it is a complex, modern concept. By our standards the plagues wrought by God through Moses upon the Egyptians were terrorist acts. So we must be careful about proof texting this issue. The Bible knows very well, however, the suffering of those who live in terror. This text, a forewarning of exile, reminds us that, ultimately, the only security we have is in God.

b. Mark 13:3-7

> *When you hear of wars and rumors of wars, do not be alarmed;*
> *this must take place, but the end is still to come.*

Do not be alarmed? Is Jesus kidding? The "little apocalypse" of Mark 13 presents Jesus discussing the end of the age and the things that must take place prior to the end. Among those things are wars and rumors of wars. What appears to be a cavalier attitude toward war by Jesus must be set in its proper eschatological context. Jesus does not minimize the suffering caused by war, but reminds his hearers that God's glory is so great that it will overshadow even war. The end of all things, remember, is not an event but a person, Jesus Christ, "coming in clouds with great power and glory."

c. Revelation 1:9

I, John, your brother who share with you in Jesus the persecution
and the kingdom and the patient endurance, ...

John says he is brother to the people of the seven churches to whom he is writing. Why? Because he shares in their suffering. How? In Jesus. Yes. Jesus died for John and the people of the seven churches, and Jesus died for us, and that makes us blood brothers and sisters. As Kierkegaard said, "Even when temporal suffering weighs down most heavily, yet the blessedness of the eternal weighs up to more."[5]

d. Psalm 120

Too long have I had my dwelling among those who hate peace.
I am for peace; but when I speak, they are for war.

It is not only soldiers and statesmen who are at risk during times of political turmoil and war. Suffering often falls most heavily on ordinary people. Those who love peace and serve the Prince of Peace are, like the psalmist, in exile among those who love war. When war envelopes us, we need more than ever the church as an embassy of peace, where we can remember who we are and act accordingly.

Other texts: Psalm 55:20-22, Isaiah 26:12, Ezekiel 13:8-16, Mark 13:1-13, and John 20:24-29.

2. Assassination and Murder

a. Exodus 20:13

Thou shalt not kill. (KJV)

At the beginning of the film *2001: A Space Odyssey*, two groups of apes engage in their traditional form of battle: they jump up and down and scream at one another, until one group frightens the other off. Then one of the defeated apes picks up a cudgel, bangs it against the ground, and has an idea. When his (I assume) group makes its next attack, they are armed with these weapons, and instead of just jumping and shouting, they bash their enemies with the clubs until they have killed them. The film suggests this was a portentous moment in our evolution. Perhaps. We would have discovered murder sooner or later, as Cain did. We were slower to discover that murder is wrong. God put the words right in our face, and still we did not listen. How long until we do?

b. Acts 23

In the morning the Jews joined in a conspiracy and bound themselves
by an oath neither to eat nor drink until they had killed Paul.
There were more than forty who joined in this conspiracy.

Murder is often a crime of passion; assassination generally has political, even religious, motivations. I have never heard a sermon preached from Acts 23, which details the intrigue in which some sought to kill Paul and others sought to preserve his life. Those who seek to compel others to believe as they do, even to the point of killing them, do something that Jesus never did. People have the right to reject the gospel. Shake the dust from your feet, yes; take up arms, no.

c. Psalm 10

They sit in ambush in the villages;
in hiding places they murder the innocent....
They think in their heart, "God has forgotten,
he has hidden his face, he will never see it."

The wrongheaded rationale of assassins, whether they operate for hire or with fanatical motives, throws us into confusion. We pray, with the psalmist, that God will arise in the midst of our confusion and bring the order to our lives that only God can bring.

Other texts: Genesis 4:8-9, 1 Kings 21, Job 24:13-17, Psalm 11:1-3, Mark 12:1-12, and 1 John 3:11-18.

3. *Economic Upheaval and Uncertainty*

a. Numbers 14:1-4

"Would that we had died in the land of Egypt! ... Why is the LORD
bringing us into this land to fall by the sword?"

The danger to the Israelites in this text was purportedly those "giants" who inhabited the land in front of them. But notice how they couched their complaint in terms of security. "We were better off as slaves in the land of Egypt." Many oppressed persons, abused spouses and others, end up preferring a known situation, however bad, to an unknown, fearful one. When our lives and livelihoods are endangered or disrupted, our faith is also at risk. What Moses told the people then is true today, "God is still with us." A friend in dire straits wrote to me concerning his uncertain future. Amidst all the uncertainly, he said, he took comfort in those things that remained strong: the love of his family, the faith of the church, and the ultimate hope he has in God.

b. Amos 8:1-6

GOD said, "Amos, what do you see?"
And I said, "A basket of summer fruit."

Amos saw a basket of summer fruit, and God said, "The end has come upon my people Israel; I will never again pass them by." As quickly as summer fruit ripens and then rots, so will Israel's days of blessing come to an end. During hard times, people long for good times; during good times, people forget what it was like to be hungry. The key here is to remember that good fortune may only be temporary, but God's love endures forever.

c. Acts 11:27-30

The disciples determined that according to their ability,
each would send relief to the believers living in Judea.

The millennia-old task of the church, caring for those in need, once again has come to the fore. I remember arguing, in the sixties, that the government was better able to care for those in dire economic circumstances than was the church. However, if, as all the politicians seem to be saying, the era of big government is over, then who is to care for those dealt crippling blows by the vicissitudes of life? While people are debating this question, others are suffering. At least we can begin with our own—no one in this congregation shall go hungry or without shelter while the rest of us can do something about it. Then we can reach out toward others. We cannot help all who are in need. But we can help some.

d. Psalm 39:12

> *Hear my prayer, O LORD, and give ear to my cry....*
> *For I am your passing guest, an alien, like all my forebears.*

The alien, the stranger, the sojourner in our midst—without power or position. Especially in the borderlands, these are the people most at risk of suffering and injustice. We must remember that we are all sojourners and pilgrims, here for a brief time at God's good pleasure. There is, in the long run, no difference between the family who lives in a nice house on the hill and the one huddled in a leaky boat seeking to escape poverty and oppression. Except one. The first family bears a responsibility for the second and will someday be called to account for what they did or did not do to help their "neighbors."

Other texts: Proverbs 30:7-9, Lamentations 1, Mark 12:41-44, and Revelation 18.

II. CONGREGATIONAL CRISES

1. Local Tragedies

Tragedy can strike the local faith community as well as the larger community. Terrible accidents can kill or maim church members. The church family can also fall victim to such heinous acts as murder, rape, abuse, or other crimes. When a death occurs, funeral sermons seek to give voice to both grief and faith.[6] But the funeral is often not the place for extended interpretation. In the Sunday sermon the pastor may deal in more depth with questions of theodicy, anger, desire for vengeance, hopelessness, and others.

a. Jeremiah 8:11

> *They have healed the wound of my people carelessly,*
> *saying 'Peace, peace,' when there is no peace.*

People in pain are not helped by having their pain discounted, by being told everything is all right when it is not all right. In this regard, Richard and Janice Lord, in their ministry with victims of crime, have assembled a description of things victims want to say to clergy. Here are the headings from that list: "Do not explain; do not take away my reality; help me deal with forgiveness with integrity; stay close; remember me ... for a long time; do not be frightened by my anger; listen to my doubt; be patient; remind me this is not all there is to life."[7]

b. Mark 15:34

> *At three o'clock Jesus cried out with a loud voice,*
> *"Eloi, Eloi, lema sabachthani?" which means,*
> *"My God, my God, why have you forsaken me?"*

Jesus' cry from the cross still hurts. In extreme situations you return to what you know, and Jesus knew scripture, quoting from Psalm 22.

In times of tragedy we may also feel confused, lost, forsaken. To what do we return for help? As pastors we may have to help our people and ourselves remember who we are and that nothing can finally separate us from the love of God (Romans 8:38-39).

c. 1 Corinthians 13

> *Love never ends.*

Dylan Thomas wrote:

> *"Though lovers be lost love shall not;*
> *And death shall have no dominion."*[8]

This poetic reprise of Romans 6:5-11 reminds us that death, which has been called the strongest moral force in the universe apart from God,[9] is just that: strong, but no match for God and for God's love.

d. Psalm 91

> *He will deliver you from the snare of the fowler*
> *and from the deadly pestilence.*

In college I studied under a dear but demanding religion professor named George Fowler. We approached his exams with a prayer from Psalm 91: "Deliver us, O Lord, from the snare of the Fowler!" What was humorous for us has been deadly serious for so many down through the centuries. This marvelous psalm gives assurance of God's protection in many threatening situations. Those "who abide in the shelter of the Almighty" will be given not only protection but also salvation.

Other texts: Jeremiah 26:16, Ezekiel 13:10-13, Matthew 5:4, and Psalms 23, 44, and 59.

2. Division and Discord

a. Proverbs 6:16-19

> *[These are among the] things that the LORD hates:*
> *. . . a lying witness who testifies falsely,*
> *and one who sows discord in a family.*

Six things the Lord hates; seven are an abomination to God. The list gains force with each one named, until it reaches the apex, or the nadir: those who sow discord among brothers and sisters. God really dislikes that. There are few things more discouraging than church strife, person against person or group against group, with the pastor often trapped on one side or the other. More people have been hated, even killed, in the name of Christ than we would like to acknowledge. How do we stop this? Are there not things worth standing up for? Yes, there are. But if we were all to admit up front that God hates discord among brothers and sisters, that it is an abomination before the Lord, then reconciliation would take its rightful important place in the discussion. Is it more important whether we have red or blue carpet or that we maintain the "unity of the Spirit in the bond of peace" (Ephesians 4:3)?

b. 1 Corinthians 1:10
Now I appeal to you, brothers and sisters, by the name of our Lord Jesus Christ, that all of you be in agreement and that there be no divisions among you, but that you be united in the same mind and the same purpose.

At a recent General Assembly of the Christian Church (Disciples of Christ), the parade of banners from new congregations presented me with one surprise. There walked a person carrying the banner of the One Mind Christian Church! I was astonished. Several of us laughed, never having been part of such a church in our lives. Was it an oxymoron? Not necessarily. I remember hearing of one church where no decisions are made unless they are unanimous. Perhaps this one is like that. It sounds strange in these divisive times, and they may fail, but at least here is one group of Christians who have pledged, through the name they carry, to do their very best to have among themselves "the mind of Christ" (1 Corinthians 2:16). They are to be honored for the attempt.

c. Psalm 109:8

Let his days be few;
and let another take his office. (KJV)

I was a guest in another city when, after church, a young man handed me a slip of paper. It had a scripture notation on it. He said with a snarl that it applied to the current President of the United States. All I had to see was "Psalm 109" to know where the young man stood. One of the imprecatory psalms, Psalm 109 is perhaps the most caustic piece of writing in the whole Bible. The psalmist's enemies are excoriated, and God's harshest judgment is called down upon them. There is one saving grace that applies not only to this but also to many other psalms of anger and lament that one could use. The psalmist says these things *to God*. As Walter Harrelson has said, it is better to pray to God for vengeance against our enemies than to take vengeance into our own hands.[10] The young man who handed me the reference was misreading the Psalms, as so many do. Take your problems with people to God. God can handle them. When you are really angry, pray—in a shout if necessary!

Other texts: Genesis 3:14-19 and 27:1-46, Matthew 12:22-32, Luke 12:49-53, Acts 28:23-28, Galatians 5:16-25, and Philippians 4:1-3.

3. Scandal and Financial Distress

Most scandals within the church, like those within the secular world, involve money, sex, or power. These are very difficult to engage from the pulpit. The preacher, as well as the people, may well find the subjects very uncomfortable. The Hebrew scriptures contain many stories about sexual misconduct: Lot's incest with his daughters in Genesis 19, Judah's sex with his daughter-in-law in Genesis 38, the Benjaminites' rape and murder of the Levite's concubine in Judges 19, David's adultery with Bathsheba in 2 Samuel 11, and Amnon's rape of Tamar in 2 Samuel 13, to mention a few. Money scandals are recorded in 2 Kings 5, John 2, and 1 Timothy 6, among other places. King David, the apostle Paul, and Jesus fell victim several times to others' power plays. These stories are not in scripture for our entertainment, but to show us the suffering that resulted from such misconduct. Suffering for the people immediately involved, the family, the tribe, even the nation. There is probably no need to use one of these stories to call people's attention to a scandal. Grapevines function at the speed of light, and people already know. What is needed is the acknowledgment of pain and direction toward healing.

a. Exodus 32:1-14

> *[Aaron] took the gold from them, formed it in a mold,*
> *and cast an image of a calf; and they said, "These are your gods,*
> *O Israel, who brought you up out of the land of Egypt!"*

They Israelites knew better, but they did it anyway. We also know better, so why do we continue to build golden calves to worship? Think about what has become your own golden calf, that which keeps you from worshiping God. God was very angry with the Israelites and prepared to destroy them, but Moses interceded with God for them, and God spared them. When we see people engaged in "idolatry," we are called, not to attack them, but to intercede with God for them.

b. 2 Samuel 13:1-22

> *Absalom hated Amnon,*
> *because he had raped his sister Tamar.*

I sat in church once and heard the pastor preach on the rape of Tamar and the subsequent revenge murder of Amnon. He went on to suggest that what we need here is forgiveness and reconciliation. We achieve this by putting the pain on Christ. I appreciated his effort, but felt that his treatment trivialized what Phyllis Trible has called a "text of terror."[11] Moving directly from the horror of the events to the forgiveness and reconciliation we have in Christ may not only be unrealistic and painful to hear, it also trivializes the power of evil among us. Evil is very real and very strong. The key, in this text and in our lives, is that evil does not have the last word.

c. Acts 5:1-11

> *But a man named Ananias, with the consent of his wife Sapphira,*
> *sold a piece of property;*
> *with his wife's knowledge, he kept back some of the proceeds,*
> *and brought only a part and laid it at the apostles' feet.*

The story about Ananias and Sapphira has become a joke these days, evoking laughter when the preacher threatens to preach a "give or die" sermon. I admit that I do not like this text and I do not think it is funny, but I am forced by canon to take it seriously. One lesson is inescapable. What appear to be money problems in the church may in fact be faith problems. Is our problem a lack of money or a lack of faith?

d. 1 Corinthians 1:18-25

> *For Jews demand signs and Greeks desire wisdom, but we proclaim*
> *Christ crucified, a stumbling block to Jews and foolishness to Gentiles.*

The words "stumbling block" literally mean "scandal." Christ crucified was a scandal to the wise and religious. At the merest hint of scandal these days, we, like our forebears, are quick to crucify. Nikos Kazantzakis told of a boy in his hometown who was nicknamed "Judas" by an insensitive teacher. The child was scarred for life.[12] Patience, compassion, and forgiveness can help many recover from their mistakes.

e. Psalm 32

> *I acknowledged my sin to you, and I did not hide my iniquity;*
> *I said, "I will confess my transgressions to the LORD";*
> *then you forgave the guilt of my sin.*

Some people will never forgive, themselves or others. That God can and will forgive our sins is the very foundation upon which faith is built. Pastors should not be too hasty to demand that injured persons forgive their tormentors, lest they compound the injury.[13] But pastors can help the church to be an agent of God's forgiveness.

Other texts: Genesis 6:5-8, Numbers 25:6-9 (a challenging text!), 2 Samuel 12:7-15, 1 Kings 15:9-15, Ecclesiastes 5:10, Matthew 1:18-25 and 21:12-17, Luke 12:13-34 and 18:9-14, and 1 Timothy 6:6-10.

III. PERSONAL CRISES

People often forget that we are sometimes forced, as Fred Craddock once said, to climb into the pulpit out of the wreckage of our own lives.[14] We may concurrently be suffering from a failure of imagination. At times like that, maybe all we can do is tell Bible stories. That is all right. These stories were helpful to people long before we added our own bit of interpretative wisdom. Many preachers, in times of personal crisis, give up and quit their ministries. This is not for me to judge, but I can say that some of the very best pastors are those who struggled through, endured the crisis, and came out the stronger for it. I am not recommending that one seek to enter crisis for its tempering quality. I tried that when I was younger, deliberately placing myself in a situation of suffering because I had heard a theologian say that his theology grew out of his own suffering. What I found was that suffering is horribly miserable and enervating. I respect ascetics like Simeon Stylites; I do not recommend that people imitate them. Suffering comes; it does not have to be sought.

Daniel Hans has identified four characteristics that need to be present when we try to preach through our own pain: vulnerability, honesty, hope, and patience. He also shares a prayer given to him by a young woman: "Dear God, teach us to laugh again, but never let us forget that we have cried."[15]

1. Loss (or threat of loss) of Employment

a. Numbers 20

> But the LORD said to Moses and Aaron, "Because you
> did not trust in me, to show my holiness before the eyes of the
> Israelites, therefore you shall not bring this
> assembly into the land which I have given them."

After all that Moses had done—leading the recalcitrant Israelites out of Egypt—now, for what seems to be a quite petty offense—striking a rock with a stick—he is not to be allowed to complete the mission for which he was called. When we find our own mission in ministry interrupted or cut short, it can be very discouraging. Moses' response to his own termination offers an extraordinary lesson, very different from that of the priest Eli in 1 Samuel. What did Eli do? Nothing. What did Moses do? He kept working. So should we, however and wherever we can.

b. 2 Corinthians 11:1-11

> I think that I am not in the least inferior to these super-apostles.
> I may be untrained in speech, but not in knowledge.

It seems that some pastors zoom up the ecclesiastical ladder, while others struggle in positions of lesser prestige and salary. On the one hand, we remember that preachers are called, not to success, but to faithful service. But on the other, pangs of jealousy may be hard to avoid. Paul complained; why can we not? Yes, Paul complained, but he was not particularly proud of that. The other lesson from him is the better one. If we lack certain talents that people appreciate, such as speaking well, then let us develop those talents that we do have: discernment, caregiving, evangelism, whatever. We can improve on our weaknesses, true; but while doing so, we can also use our natural gifts to the maximum. The church has a need for the gifts we have. We must look for the right place to use them.

c. Psalm 46:1-2

> *God is our refuge and strength, a very present help in trouble.*
> *Therefore we will not fear, though the earth should change,*
> *though the mountains shake in the heart of the sea.*

Many people, especially men, tend to identify themselves with their work. I do not do my job; I am my job. In times of company downsizing and shifting employment bases, many are caught in the net, pulled from their familiar waters, and cast aside. And some of those lose not just their jobs, but also their identities. We must help them to hear, though their circumstances change and their world turns upside down, how God dearly loves them and will be their refuge and strength until they are back on their own feet again. Then they, wounded healers, can help others to hear the same thing.

Other texts: Nehemiah 6:1-5, Ecclesiastes 2:23, Philippians 3:12-16, and 2 Timothy 4:6-8.

2. Family Problems:
Illness, Accident, Separation, Divorce, Death

The ministers of God are not immune to the troubles of this world. Our marriages fall apart. Our children use drugs. Other tragedies befall us. Often, when we are in crisis, our congregations in their mercy remove the burden of the pulpit from us. Sometimes, however, magnificent sermons have been preached by persons in crisis, none greater that I know of than Gossip's "But when life tumbles in, what then?" following the unexpected death of his wife. Fosdick put it correctly when he said: "Crisis can call out great hours."[16] We do not wear our pain on our sleeves when in the pulpit. If our purpose is making the congregation feel sorry for us, we will succeed in that, but not in preaching. Preaching in personal crisis requires courage and a certain equanimity, that we can focus our attention on the word God has for all of us and not just our own misery. This is a difficult task. It is also a great witness when our people can hear a word of hope from one who can call back across the waves, with Hopeful, "I have touched the bottom and it is sound."[17]

a. 1 Samuel 2:12-25

Now the sons of Eli were scoundrels; they had no regard
for the LORD.... [Eli] said to them, "Why do you do such things?
For I hear of your evil dealings from all the people." ...
But they would not listen to the voice of their father.

One of the saddest stories in scripture is that of Eli, priest at Shiloh. His two sons are a disappointment to him, but Eli, who has grown insensitive over the years, is unable to deal with it. Later God tells the boy Samuel in a vision that Eli's days as priest are over. Eli receives the news with an air of fatalism and later falls over and dies. No one that I know would call their children "worthless," as Eli's were called, but many have dealt with children who "would not listen to the voice of their father" or mother. Often there are no simple answers. This is no fundamentalist appeal to "keep your family in subjection," but notice the one thing that Eli did not do: the priest did not go to God with his problem. Time and love, yes. Counseling, if need be. But we who preach the power of prayer should not ignore prayer when dealing with our own problems.

b. Matthew 14:6-20

Now when Jesus heard this, he withdrew from there in a
boat to a deserted place by himself. But when the crowds heard it,
they followed him on foot from the towns.

It is hard to know how Jesus responded to the deaths of those he loved. There are but few mentioned in the Gospels. On several occasions he raised people from the dead, even his friend Lazarus, over whom he wept. But when John the Baptist was beheaded, Jesus was mute. He did two things, however, which are instructive to us. First, he went apart to a lonely place, which, as we know from other readings, means that he went to pray. Second, he gave attention to those who remained, in this case the hungry people who had followed him. Prayer and community are the rock upon which we stand when the storms of this world come upon us. When Charlie Shedd found himself both angry and discouraged following the death of his wife, he made these affirmations: "(1) I refuse to drown in self-pity; ... (2) I will not talk too much; ... (3) I will get help from the right people; ... (4) I will do something for others; ... and (5) I will get ready ahead of time."[18]

c. Psalm 16:1-2
> *Protect me, O God, for in you I take refuge.*
> *I say to the LORD, "You are my Lord;*
> *I have no good apart from you.*

Are there any wrenchings more painful than those that tear families apart? When this occurs in the parsonage, there is a double portion of pain. People may say, "I thought they were supposed to model relationship for us; and they cannot even keep their own relationship together," not terribly unlike those of another time who said, "If you are the Son of God, come down from the cross." Fortunately, most people understand how difficult it is to maintain relationships within the strains of ministry and are caring and supportive. The bottom line, though, is that of this text. When our family and our world fall apart, help us, O God, not to fall also apart from you.

Other texts: Isaiah 40:1-2, Matthew 2:16-18, Mark 5:1-20,

Romans 8:28-38, 2 Corinthians 1:3-7 and 12:1-10, and 1 Thessalonians 4:13-18.

3. Depression or Loss of Faith

Some people and some ministers become psychologically and theologically dysfunctional. Sometimes the dysfunction is cool; sometimes it is hot. In his autobiography, William Maxwell, longtime editor of *The New Yorker*, described his own position as "simply an unbelief. A negative. If you could only develop a print from it you would have saving faith."[19] The pain of unbelief and the consequent wonder at belief are shown in these next lines of Maxwell's:

> I came across a [story] about a man named John F. M. Parker, and in it were these two sentences: "Within eleven months he lost a son, a daughter, his farm and his wife. But then he said: 'I know whom I have believed, and am persuaded that He is able to keep that which I have committed to Him against that day.'" It makes me hang my head in shame.[20]

How does one get from the unbelief and shame of Maxwell to the faith of Parker? One step and one day at a time.

a. Jeremiah 20:7-13
> For the word of the LORD has become for me
> a reproach and derision all day long.

Jeremiah is sick—of everything. He no longer wants to preach. The six personal laments included in the book of Jeremiah give witness to this. Most of us have been there, where the preparation and delivery of sermons have become a great ordeal. We feel we have nothing to say and no way to say it. Jeremiah goes on to say that there is within his heart "a burning fire." Word of God? Indigestion? Sometimes it is hard to say. And yet, in spite of his discouragement with preaching, Jeremiah admits that he is weary with holding it in—whatever "it" is—and he cannot. When we find ourselves in places where we no longer trust ourselves and our own interpretative powers, trust that Word which was and is and is to come. Preach it, as one person said, until you believe it again.

b. Isaiah 6:1-8

> *Woe is me! I am lost, for I am a man of unclean lips,*
> *and I live among a people of unclean lips.*

What made Isaiah feel so bad? He was apparently feeling rather average until that fateful line: "I saw the Lord sitting on a throne, high and lofty." We pray for the presence of God, but this shows the other side of that. In the presence of such holiness, our sin seems all the more wretched. What happened to Isaiah happens, in perhaps less dramatic fashion, to many of us. In our handling of holy things, we feel our moral failure all the more profoundly. What the angel said to Isaiah is instructive for us: "Your guilt has departed and your sin is blotted out." May the burning coal of God's mercy touch all our lips.

c. Mark 16:1-8

> *But go, tell his disciples and Peter*
> *that he is going ahead of you to Galilee;*
> *there you will see him, just as he told you.*

When a person of faith is overwhelmed with doubt, it can be devastating. The pastor's faith is for many the rock to which they cling when their own faith is in doubt. As someone once said, "If you cannot pray, I will pray for you." But when the rock itself is in danger of crumbling, everyone is in danger. And the pastor then feels not only doubt, but also guilt. "There is a hole ... where the Holy should be."[21] We resonate with the words of the country song, "When you leave that way, you can never go back. A train won't run on a torn-up track."[22] Gary Parker has outlined several sources of doubt: weak foundations, confusing observations, imperfect personification, lack of investigation, and wearying situations.[23] Four helps I know: time, friends, work, and God. First, doubt is sometimes like the wind: it comes, and then it goes. That which we cannot conquer we may be able to outlast. Second, when we are not strong, it is acceptable to lean on those who are. Let those whom you have helped help you: parishioners, friends, colleagues, family. Third, many discouragements dissipate in the catharsis of hard work. And finally, listen to this affirmation: Peter. Bumbling Peter. Peter, who spoke so stupidly on the Mount of Transfiguration, who when asked to pray cut off an ear instead, who finally denied Jesus, fell into unbelief, and wept bitterly. When the women went to the tomb of the crucified Jesus, they found the stone rolled away and an angel there, who said to them: "Go, tell his disciples and Peter." Notice. "And Peter." Peter may have lost faith in God, but God had not lost faith in Peter. God was not finished with Peter. His faith was restored, and he became the rock upon which the church was built. God has not lost faith in you. God is not finished with you. Hold on.

d. Psalm 102

> *I lie awake; I am like a lonely bird on the housetop....*
> *My days are like an evening shadow; I wither away like grass.*

The psalmist's insomnia and sense of withering are classic symptoms of depression. Nothing seems right; life drags on. Pastors and other caregivers, so quick to recognize these symptoms in others, are often unable to see them in themselves. Sheldon Kopp, a well-known psychotherapist, fell into depression while struggling with a brain tumor. Finally, he went to his own mentor and laid out his situation in clinical terms. His teacher replied, "How come a big tough guy like you is thrown by a little thing like a brain tumor?"[24] Kopp's teacher helped him to "laugh at myself for thinking that I should be able to handle anything, without sorrow, rest, or comfort."[25] New studies on depression offer hopeful approaches, from drugs to counseling. Meantime, when you find your life spinning out of control and all your coping methods fail you, please allow a friend or counselor to mediate God's love for you.

Other texts: Genesis 32:22-30, 1 Kings 19:1-18,[26] Psalm 103, Ezekiel 37:1-11, and Mark 9:23-24.

CHAPTER EIGHT
CRISIS SERMONS

t is helpful to see how other preachers have preached in crisis. No collection of sermons, however, could claim to have covered all the crises that might occur. Each crisis is unique. My collection of crisis sermons grows larger. Rather than reprint sermons that are readily available elsewhere, I list a number of them in the bibliography, offering here previously unpublished sermons which model preaching in the midst of public, congregational, and personal crises.

1. A PORTRAIT IN EBONY

A sermon preached by the Reverend Colbert S. Cartwright
at Pulaski Heights Christian Church, Little Rock, Arkansas,
September 8, 1957[1]

Bert Cartwright was one of the few White Protestant ministers in Little Rock, Arkansas, in 1957, who supported the efforts to desegregate the public schools there. He paid a price for doing so. He also consistently used the pulpit to proclaim the gospel as he understood it in the midst of this crisis. Some of the sermons were exegetical; others were doctrinal. The following sermon is more of a narrative, the story of one young Black woman who enrolled in Central High School in September 1957. The impact of the sermon reaches beyond time and place and language, and even race.

It is worth noting that three weeks after the events recounted in the sermon, federal troops escorted the Black students into Central High School. Furthermore, the fortieth anniversary of that occasion was celebrated on September 26, 1997, with President Clinton in attendance. The following brief account of that celebration is a telling counterpoint to the events of September 1957:

> Slowly, with heads held high, nine black adults climbed the steps of Central High School yesterday, paused before a hushed crowd, then turned and, one by one, strode through doors held wide open for them by the governor of Arkansas and the president of the United States.
>
> After 40 years, the Little Rock Nine now offered a new image to contrast the indelible pictures of them, as teenagers, walking silently through seething, white mobs, heading for the same schoolhouse door, having it shut in their faces.
>
> The nine were celebrated as heroes yesterday, four decades to the day after president Eisenhower deployed federal troops to escort them, finally, into this city's pre-eminent whites-only school.
>
> There was no more spit, no more jeering, no more threat of physical violence as thousands of children and adults, black and white, paid homage to their home town civil-rights pioneers.[2]

The central figure in the Reverend Cartwright's sermon, Elizabeth Eckford, now in her mid-fifties, is the only one of the Little Rock Nine who still lives in Little Rock.[3]

Scripture: Psalm 27

Wednesday morning at about ten minutes to eight o'clock I saw a slim, attractive Negro girl wearing tinted glasses, approaching the campus of Central High School. She had been enrolled by the school board at Central High as one of nine colored students to share school life with some 2,000 White students. She had gotten off the bus and had walked a block to the edge of the campus.

When she arrived at school, she saw some 135 National Guardsmen armed with rifles, billy clubs, and tear gas, awaiting her. Calmly and with poise Elizabeth Eckford sought to pass through the Guardsmen to enter her school. Waving a billy club in the air, a Guardsman, acting on the orders of Governor Faubus, directed her across the street away from the school.

Clutching her green school notebook with a bit firmer grip, she started walking down the street in front of the school building. She was a lone Negro girl in the midst of some 200 White persons who had gathered in front of the school.

As she neared the main entrance to the high school, she crossed the street to gain access to the school to which the board of education had transferred her. As she approached the sidewalk bordering the school, the armed Guardsmen drew together and blocked her from entering the school.

Now the crowd saw her. It closed in behind her, and began hurling abuses at her. Elizabeth, tight-lipped and with no sign of emotion, continued her stately walk down the two block length of Park Avenue which the school faces.

Looking neither to the right nor to the left, she silently withstood the crowd's jeers. She heard someone cry out to her, "Go back where you came from." She heard a female voice call out, "Go home before you get hurt, nigger. Why don't you go back to the ... jungle." Without rebuttal and with no outward expression of emotion, Elizabeth Eckford continued her lonely walk through the crowd.

The intensity of abuse increased: "Go back to poppa Blossom!" "Smut-nut! Stop her!" A hysterical woman, crying "Go back where you came from," lunged toward her, but was held back by a National Guardsman. Another voice shouted, "Trip her."

When Elizabeth came to the end of the block she sat down on a bench and awaited a bus to take her back home. A bus came by, but it was too crowded to pick her up. She waited with dignity for the next bus, as White persons continued to pour out their invective. After enduring the White crowd's vulgarisms for thirty-five minutes, she caught a bus home, as the White students at Central High were standing at attention for the raising of the American flag. Elizabeth would not give her pledge of allegiance to the flag of her nation "under God" that day.

The picture of a Negro high school girl in a gingham and white dress walking with dignity and composure in the face of an ugly mob is one which I shall never forget. How could a fifteen-year-old girl manage to behave in such a noble fashion? How could she keep her wits about her and her tongue silent?

Night before last I found the answer. I drove down an unpaved street in the southeast portion of Little Rock and stopped before a small frame house.

I was met at the door by Mrs. Eckford who, when she heard I was the minister of Pulaski Heights Christian Church, greeted me warmly and invited me in. The six Eckford children were all gathered in the neat but plainly furnished living room watching television. The television set was politely and firmly turned off by the mother.

I talked with Elizabeth and found her to be a reserved young woman who immediately gave you the feeling of being in the presence of a person of deep inward resources.

"Were you afraid as you walked along Park Avenue?" I asked her.

"At first I wasn't afraid," Elizabeth said. "I came to the school corner and asked the guard what time it was. He said 'six minutes to eight' and told me to cross the street. I did what he said. But then somebody right behind me said, 'Push her.' They didn't touch me, but I thought they might. I was afraid then."

"But Elizabeth, you didn't show any signs of fear," I observed.

"I was afraid I'd burst out crying, and I didn't want to in front of all that crowd." Elizabeth hadn't.

Elizabeth's mother could not help showing pride in her daughter as she recalled the incident. "I was worried, too," Mrs. Eckford confessed. "I kept my ear to the radio and heard about her being alone like that. I was relieved when she got home safe. But I knew all the time she would do what was right. I never questioned that."

I was curious about a mother's faith in her teenage daughter. "Why were you so sure?" I asked.

"The night before she went to school," Mrs. Eckford replied, "I told her to be sure and read her Bible that night and again in the morning before she started out."

"What did you read, Elizabeth?" I asked. "Do you remember?"

"I read the fourth Psalm the night before, and the twenty-seventh Psalm that morning before I caught the bus."

We got the well-worn Bible out, and I took it and turned to the twenty-seventh Psalm. As I read it aloud to the family with the little boys' eyes upturned to me from their seated position on the floor, I knew the source of Elizabeth's strength to face the most horrible and frightening moment of her life.

I began reading from the twenty-seventh Psalm [KJV]: "The LORD is my light and my salvation; whom shall I fear? the LORD is the strength of my life; of whom shall I be afraid?" I knew then that it was Elizabeth's Lord who had been the source of strength.

I read on: "When the wicked, even mine enemies and my foes, came upon me to eat up my flesh, they stumbled and fell. Though an host should encamp against me, my heart shall not fear: though war should rise against me, in this will I be confident." My mind went back to Wednesday's scene. The wicked, Elizabeth's enemies and her foes, came upon her to devour her, if possible. I saw the fully armed National Guardsmen encamped against her, blocking her way to school. I heard once more the sounds of the war-like mob vomiting the filth of a lifetime's accumulation upon her.

And then I saw the young Negro teenager walking briskly but with dignity down Park Avenue. I could picture her now with the words of the Psalmist seeping into her consciousness as she walked a walk which seemed never to end. "My heart shall not fear ... in this will I be confident."

When we completed the reading of the Psalm, I quietly closed the book. I looked into Elizabeth's eyes and asked her firmly, "Elizabeth, if you had it all to do over again and knowing what you would have to go through, would you do it again?" With the same quiet calmness that can only spring from depths of spiritual reserves, she said, "If it would do any good, I'd do it again."

Elizabeth told me that she had not decided to enter Central High until about four weeks ago. She thought about it all summer. She wants to be a lawyer. There are speech courses offered at Central that she could not get at Horace Mann. "I wanted to be as well prepared as I can be when I go to college," she explained. "I thought and thought about it."

She paused pensively for a moment, and then continued, "I remembered my pastor once saying you should take advantage of every opportunity."

I asked Elizabeth if she thought she could keep up with her classmates in Central if she were admitted. She said she was an "A and B" student and thought she could make her grades all right.

"Are you anxious to get started to school, or are you enjoying not having to go to school?" I asked. Elizabeth replied that she missed school. "If matters aren't settled in a few days will you go to Horace Mann?" "I'm not going back to Horace Mann," she said softly, but very firmly. I don't believe she will.

I felt I was imposing upon the family, and so I got up to leave. Impulsively I said to Elizabeth, "This week I've been ashamed to be a White person."

"Why?" she asked softly.

"Because," I said, "it is we White people who have caused all your troubles. I'm ashamed."

Elizabeth put out her hand to clasp mine. Shaking my hand with the same firmness she had shown in everything else she has done, she said, "No, Reverend Cartwright, it's just some of the White people who have stirred things up." There was no bitterness in her voice. She thanked me for coming over to see her.

As I walked away I could not but ask myself, "Who is *my* light and *my* salvation? who is the strength of *my* life?" I knew who the source was for Elizabeth. I wondered if I knew my Lord very well at all. What would I do in a similar circumstance?

In my book Elizabeth Eckford is one of the most noble spirits I have ever known. Central's White students are the poorer for not knowing her. If Elizabeth does not get to attend Central, whose loss will be the greater—hers or those whose hate-distorted hearts might have been transformed by knowing one who knows that "the Lord is the strength of my life"?

I have visited in the homes of the other Negro children who have been turned away by the Governor's militia. I have been impressed with the quality of these young people. Despite every reason for being bitter, they have expressed no hatred. Their only complaint is against the Governor their parents helped elect.

This morning we are all engulfed by the events that have flooded upon us during the past week. The issues involved in this situation are as momentous as they are complex. We are faced with vast issues of constitutional law. Our national government is faced with the gravest internal crisis since the Civil War. Vast political forces are tugging and pulling. Much of the solution to the problem will come about by processes in which we will have no direct part.

But the thing I want us to remember this morning is that these nine Negro high school kids are human beings. We shall be in danger of losing our own souls if, in the midst of great impersonal issues, we lose sight of some very bright children of high moral character who want an education— an education not available to them in formerly Negro schools.

When we think of the problems facing us, let us think of an Elizabeth Eckford, who has more guts than anyone present here today. Let us think of a girl who quietly read her Bible one night, and then again the next morning, and found that what the Bible said was true:

> The LORD is my light and my salvation; whom shall I fear? The LORD is the strength of my life; of whom shall I be afraid? When the wicked, even mine enemies and my foes, came upon me to eat up my flesh, they stumbled and fell. Though an host should encamp against me, my heart shall not fear: though war should rise against me in this will I be confident.

2. A MOTHER'S LAMENT

A Prayer offered by Ms. Jo Pendleton
at an ecumenical worship service held at the Central Presbyterian
Church, in Waco, Texas, on April 20, 1993, the day following the fire
that engulfed the Branch Davidian compound.[4]

While not a sermon, this prayer by a librarian makes very effective use of the twin languages of lamentation and faith. It was written very early on the morning after the conflagration and offered that same evening.

O God, the children—we weep for the children.
   The ten billion words that have been written,
   the speculations that have been made,
   the fingers of blame that have been pointed,
   all make no difference here—they are empty and
   meaningless
   as we mourn the loss of each child's life.
We have known them only from printed names in the
newspaper and an occasional photograph.
   But God you *know* them!
   I read about a twelve-year-old girl being sexually molest-
ed, and I think about my own daughters . . .
   I read about a one-year-old baby dying in the flames, and
I remember my babies—and my heart cries out!
   I read about an expectant mother dying in the flames,
and I remember the joy, the hope, the all-possible of carry-
ing new life.
   But you, God, you KNOW them.
   You have called each one by name.
   You sang out, you danced on the day that each one was
born!
   You have known them, and you have loved them with a
love far greater than we can imagine.
   As a loving parent,
      you weep with those who weep this morning,
      every grandmother,
      every grandfather,
      each brother and sister.
   You share the sorrow of every mother and father.
   We lay before you our outrage
      our terrible sadness
      our fears about our own children
   And we thank you for the healing and the grace of tears.
   For those whose hearts have hardened
      as this ordeal dragged on,

please break the hardness,
soften the protective shell that we so skillfully develop,
    and let us feel the pain of loss.
Lord, deliver us from dwelling
    on the ashes and the remains of these your children.
Lift up our eyes to you, our source of life and hope.
For the sake of thy kingdom, O God, which knows no
end. Amen.

3. THROUGH IT ALL, THERE IS GOD

A sermon preached by the Reverend Annette Sowell
at First United Methodist Church, Crowley, Texas,
on April 23, 1995.[5]

This sermon was preached during an evening service on
the National Day of Mourning following the bombing of the
federal building in Oklahoma City, Oklahoma, on April 19,
1995. It was a sermon knit together in a time of great passion
and pain for preacher and people alike. There was little time
to prepare. In crisis, the preaching challenge is often crafting,
rather than creating. Together with its other strengths, this
sermon demonstrates the crafting of source material into a
flowing, moving whole. The preacher borrowed from previous work she had done on Ezekiel, along with other contemporary sources, and then quickly and creatively shaped that
material into a fresh message of good news in a trying time.

Scripture: Ezekiel 37:1-3, 11-14

I. Introduction

His name was Ezekiel and, like Christ, he was "a man of
sorrows and acquainted with grief." When he was but a
lad, his beloved city, Jerusalem, fell. He was taken into captivity in the land of Babylon. There he slept on a mat on the

earthen floor, squatted to eat from trays, and drank beer and wine brewed from dates. He lived in a house of clay bricks with walls made very thick for insulation against the fierce heat of the plains. There were no windows, except for small ventilation holes near the ceiling.

Then God called him to be a prophet. And he became a man known for his strange and puzzling visions. His writings are a wonderful and confusing blend of beautiful poetry and hard to understand prose. His visions are a mix of the past and a hint of the future. The vision we have just read is one of those. He sees a vision: a valley of dry bones. And God makes those bones live again. God puts God's own spirit within the dead, dry bones and they live.

The point of the vision? It is this: for all of us for whom existence has become for all intents and purposes a grave—there is hope in the Almighty promises.... For all of us who reel from the terror of the bombing in America's heartland—there is hope in the Almighty promises.... I will put my spirit within you, and you will live. For through it all, there is God.

II. The *Why?* Question

Almost always the first question we ask in a tragedy of any kind and certainly in a tragedy of this magnitude is, Why? Why did this happen? And I say to you, all indications so far are that this happened for no good reason. Bad things happen to the good and to the bad all the time.

> The notion that only good things happen to good people was put to rest when they hung Jesus on the cross.... God's love carries no promises about good or bad save the promise that God will not allow anything worse to happen to us than happened to his own Son.[6]

And that, should we die, like him we will be resurrected to eternal life with God. And so on this national day of mourning for the tragedy and the terror in America's heart-land, we come to mourn, to remember, to pray for mercy and healing. And to receive not answers but comfort and courage to trust in a God who promises to put God's own spirit within us that we might live, for through it all, there is God.

III. For "The Little Ones"

There is much in this world that threatens us. There are neonatal intensive care units today in Oklahoma and all across America that nurse and treasure America's most precious little ones and watch them lose their battle to live. "There are respirators that must be unplugged. There are courthouses hearing case after case of child abuse, divorce, human destructiveness at its finest. There are classrooms where children have knives and guns and drugs." There are places in this world where innocent people are imprisoned just because they crossed an invisible land boundary by mistake. "There are places in this world . . . where children go to bed hungry and old people wander away from their villages to die—ashamed of their helplessness and feeling hopeless."[7]

But know this!!!

Jesus knows the pain in this world.

Jesus knows the challenges that sit before us.

Jesus knows that there are those who weave webs of destruction and desperation for themselves and for others.

And so Jesus sends doctors and nurses into neonatal ICU units and rescue workers into bombed-out buildings and policemen into the debris of a daycare center, so they can hand out to firefighters sent by God the little ones who have suffered and already been taken to heaven.

Jesus sends an amateur photographer to snap a picture that the world might be forever reminded that there are more good people in this world than bad people.

Jesus sends dedicated teachers and administrators into classrooms to teach children that knives and guns and drugs are not the way to live and breathe the spirit of God.

Jesus sends the Red Cross and the Feed the Children Foundation to feed and care for the children and their families.

Oh, yes, through it all, there is God. God with skin on, in the good people who go out in the name of Jesus to give living water to those who thirst. Through it all, there is God with skin on, in the good people who mourn with those who mourn and hold the hands and hearts of those who sit and wait for the news that will never come now, those who sit and wait for the final moment when they know they can now plan a funeral instead of a celebration.

And, make no mistake about it ... through it all, there is God, sitting in a jail cell on a military base in Oklahoma, with a man who will be punished by the laws of this land. Our God weeps for us all. And, if we are to breathe with the spirit of God, we, too, must weep for this man and his associates, whoever they are. And we must forgive, when we can, the great pain and anguish he has let loose on our nation, our children, our families, throughout America. If we do not weep for him, too, if we do not struggle toward forgiveness, will there be room in us for the breath of God to fill us that we might live?

IV. Conclusion

The day of the devastating bombing that shook our land this week will long be remembered, by those whose lives were destroyed by it, by those of us who watched the camera crews and the reporters describe the scene, by those of us who watched little Baylee in the arms of the firefighter, who begged, "Breathe, baby, breathe." We will never forget.

And, please God, we will remember the goodness of people that poured from around the world as the spirit of God breathed into us all a new life and a new spirit of determination, of commitment, of forgiveness. Let us also remember that where God's all-powerful gospel is faithfully proclaimed and totally believed, where believers undergird and intercede for each other, where the Holy Spirit is earnestly sought to breathe spiritual life into persons involved, there the miracles of God will take place again and again.

The valley of dry bones will become a living army of conquerors, standing tall on their feet by the grace of Almighty God.[8] It took place for Ezekiel. It can take place for each of us and for all of those in the heartland of America. For through it all, there is always God. Amen.

Congregational Hymn:
Through it all,
Through it all,
I've learned to trust in Jesus,
I've learned to trust in God;
Through it all,
Through it all,
I've learned to depend upon God's word.[9]

4. TRUTH HEALS

A sermon preached by the Reverend Dr. J. Philip Wogaman
at the Foundry United Methodist Church, Washington, D.C.
September 20, 1992

The preacher of the following sermon accepted a call to the pastorate of the venerable Foundry United Methodist Church and began his ministry there in June of 1992. Dr. Wogaman was one of only five persons at that time who knew that his predecessor, who had served the church for twenty-seven years, had been charged by two women with sexual misconduct. Agreements involving confidentiality were reached but fell apart when further information became known. On Monday, September 14, a letter on the matter was mailed to all church members. The following Sunday Dr. Wogaman preached this sermon, which he described as "the most difficult sermon of my life" to a congregation in crisis.[10]

In the sermon, the preacher helps his people to distinguish between truth and fact, and then offers several perspectives on the truth in their current situation. Pastoral and prophetic, the sermon both aches and affirms. The preacher interprets the past *sub specie aeternitatis*, provides a landscape where the pain of the situation can be placed, and points to a hopeful future of care and service.

Scripture: John 8:31-32, 14:1-10

I do not often, or lightly, change a sermon topic or scripture that has been announced in advance. This has appeared to be one of those weeks when I should do so. The new sermon topic was suggested to me by a remark made by one of the members of the administrative board last Monday night. In the midst of our discussion, as many points of view and feelings were being expressed, she said: "Remember: only the truth heals."

"Only the truth heals." That brought to mind a part of the scripture today, "You will know the truth and the truth will make you free." And I find myself asking, "Could that really be? The truth heals? The truth makes you free? Are there not truths that hurt, cruel truths, hard truths? What could it mean that the truth heals?" Searching for an answer, we first turn to our other scripture in John which raises the question, "What is truth?"

What *is* truth? I have to confess I am not thoroughly pleased with some of the words John chose. Perhaps I am offended that John did not consult me. I freely acknowledge that none of my writings have been canonized. So we shall have to make do with John's: "I am the way and the truth and the life. No one comes to the Father except through me. If you know me you will know my father also. From now on you do know him and have him. . . . If you continue in my word you are truly my disciples. You will know the truth. The truth will make you free."

Let's bracket off questions having to do with whether non-Christians can be saved (which I strongly believe) and issues of theological language, and proceed to the heart of the matter. What is truth? Truth to John is Jesus Christ as revealer of God. In John we read that the word became flesh and dwelt among us, full of grace, truth, peace, justice. In Jesus Christ we see what God is up to. We see what God is like. And all that we might say about grace infusing human life and defining and gathering us, all of that is implied in these words. God is truth, not just a truth:

- God the very center and source of all being, in whom we live and move and have our being.
- God who has given us the gift of life.
- God who in Christ has given us the gift of grace.

God is truth to us. Now that raises the question of how we shall deal with the relationship between truth and fact. We often use the words interchangeably. But truth is not fact. Nor is truth to be confused with mere accuracy. Even accurate facts can mislead or deceive. Journalists know that well. I also must say I know it even better after interacting with some journalists through the week. A journalist is called to the high task of separating out those facts that are decisive in interpreting the truth. So must we bear in mind that the interpretation we bring to the factual world is what is decisive in our understanding of truth about the world. Truth contains the core, the essence, the nub, the heart of the matter. To John the truth containing the core, the essence, the nub, the heart of the matter is God as revealed in Jesus Christ. I have just finished the writing of a book, a history of Chrisitan ethics. If I ever had any doubt about the importance of selectivity of fact, I do not now. Out of all that vast canvas of human history and Christian reflection upon it I, humble servant that I am, have to decide what the reader will consider to be important truth, an awesome responsibility.

Truth then is not just fact. Fact can obscure truth. Truth is the interpretation of fact. In Jesus Christ we have the clue to interpret truth. We do sometimes seek to evade the truth because we do not have a sufficient grasp upon the source of truth. To look at it in a humorous personal way: every morning when we get up and look in the mirror we see facts which may not be entirely to our choosing, and we may seek to rearrange the facts more thoughtfully. Every culture is like this. Every human being is like this. Nothing wrong with that. Just don't mistake the rearrangement for ultimate truth.

I wonder now about the situation we are confronting. You may wonder how much to share with whom. We affirm that we are an open church, a receptive church, that all are welcome. We do not hide anything. We are decent. We understand that the truth is deeper than facts, and we summon people to see the deeper perspective. But in a situation like this you wonder how to speak to your friends and children and others. I cannot answer that question for you. I can say that, as in a family, it is probably a mistake to be deeply concerned yourself, and yet to withhold what that means to those who are close to you (bearing in mind that the way things are shared must always be age specific and helpful to people at the time and place of their need). I am not a professional psychiatrist nor do I intend to be an amateur one, but I think that is psychological wisdom. To be open, to let the healing start from the ground, from the bottom.

Organizations like Alcoholics Anonymous have helped us to understand the importance of that. You know how the testimonies begin in Alcoholics Anonymous meetings, "I am so and so. I am an alcoholic." That comes from persons who may not have touched a drop in years but nevertheless recognize that this is a part of the reality of their lives and that they still need help. That company of people, Alcoholics Anonymous, based as it is upon God's grace, has been enormously helpful to people, especially at the point of their acknowledgment of who they are and what they need. And is that not true for all of us? We have to touch base with the bottom, where we learn that the God of grace has been there before us, the God who lifts us and helps us grow together.

Now what are we to say about what has happened in our midst in the church? If the truth heals and if it is God's truth that heals, what are we to say? Clearly the first truth is the truth about each one of us, that we are God's children. Sometimes I find myself reflecting—what are the facts about my life that I would not want anybody to use to define me? What are those facts? In my case I can think of one or two . . . hundred. On the other hand, what are the facts about our lives that we would like to have to define us? I can think of one or two. Period. But the fact that does define us is that we belong to God. That is the fact. We belong to the God who knows all of the other facts and who is there to help us in grace. What freedom, what healing there is in knowing that God already knows it all and that we go to God who is the source of our grace. Truth number one.

The second truth has to do with the feelings and the attitudes that we bring to this kind of situation. Your staff here at the church has been very busy through this week talking with many people in the congregation. I figured out that I have personally talked with two or three hundred, either individually or in small groups, all over our parish. I'm an expert on the conflicting emotions and feelings and attitudes that are here. I've heard it from so many in the parish, and they mirror my feelings. And indeed the conflicting feelings run through each of us. It is not very good advice to suppress those feelings. One remembers that Arabian proverb: "A friend is one to whom one may pour out all of the contents of one's heart, chaff and grain together, knowing that the gentlest of hands will take it and hold all that is good, and with the breath of kindness blow the rest away."[11] And I find myself thinking "what a friend we have in Jesus." God is our friend. God is like that. Don't suppress the feelings. You can't go around them. You've got to go through them.

One of the problems with abuses in the counseling relationship is that it may make it more difficult for people to face their feelings honestly and to understand them and to grow through them. Therefore a third truth has to do with the damage, the harm, the hurt, bearing in mind that everybody is hurt in situations of this kind. We think of my predecessor and his family. What an avalanche of prayer has gone up from this church this week and now for them. Think also of the women who are involved. They too need an avalanche of prayer and understanding. We're learning a lot more about how these situations develop in the lives of people, the harm that can be done, and what may be needed to heal. We know that women in so many areas of life have suffered silently in our culture. We have to resolve as a culture, as a whole society, that this has got to stop, so the hurt doesn't continue to be silent. We think of all the people, everybody in the church, who are hurt. Part of the truth is that there is much hurt here.

A fourth truth has to do with the ministry of the last twenty-seven years. This truth is that very great good has come to large numbers of people. It is God's good working through human channels to help us all. Do not say no to that. Do not submerge that. That is truth. That is a part of God's truth. I want to confess to you that when I first stood in this pulpit and enjoyed the enormous privilege of preaching to this great congregation I knew a lot about what you now know. It had been shared pursuant to agreements between all of the parties, with an understanding of confidentiality at a time when it was not known whether this would become public, and I carried the weight of that, along with a very small number of others in the congregation. And what I want you to know is that when I spoke on that occasion about the history of this church, and specifically about the history of the last twenty-seven years in this church, everything I said then I would say again now. Do not feel that you need to rewrite history. You can never rewrite history. That history is in your soul. The only way you can rewrite history is to say no to a part of yourself. That is part of the truth.

And I think I also want to add the truth of the integrity of the leadership of this church. I have marveled in these months now at the quality of that leadership, and I don't mean just the ability to lead. I mean the ability to lead with integrity, compassion, and Christian depth. And what do I mean by the leadership of this church? Not some elite. I mean all of the people of this church, because everybody here is a leader in some aspect of our life together. I want to reaffirm my confidence in the leadership of this church.

Now the final truth that comes to me this morning is that, as we lift our eyes above the horizon of this sadness and these events in our midst, we see how God is brooding over this church and is setting us in mission. God has a very important agenda for this church. Here we are situated at one of the great intersections of modern life, in the heart of a great city, in the heart of the nation's capital, with a voice to the world, to the nation, to our community, to ourselves. God has high hopes for this church, great dreams for this church. If we work together as Christians in mission we will experience those hopes and those dreams. One of the wonderful things about the history of this church, in at least the last decades and probably long before, is the great diversity of this church. What that diversity means is that people of all kinds are welcome here and feel welcome here and because of that we can be a mission to a world in which many people do not feel welcome, a world of injustice and tragedy and hopelessness. That word to us from God this morning is we have work to do together in this church.

And what is the last word? The last word doesn't come from human beings. But the last word of this sermon will be from the gospel of Luke, a word which comes to all of us together. "Fear not little flock, it is God's good pleasure to give you the kingdom" (12:32). And may the grace of the Lord Jesus Christ be with us all. Amen.

5. TO EVERYTHING A SEASON

A sermon preached by the Reverend Gina Rhea
at the First Christian Church, Radford, Virginia
May 1, 1988[12]

The following sermon was preached on the first Sunday after a marital separation had occurred between the author and her husband. The two had served together as co-pastors for eight and a half years in the congregation where the sermon was delivered. On the previous Sunday evening, the co-pastors met with the elders to announce their separation. At the meeting the author's husband resigned the co-pastorate, effective immediately, and the author expressed her desire to renegotiate the call with the congregation in order to remain as the pastor. The elders, in a unanimous recommendation to the Official Board, affirmed her desire to remain. A letter from the co-pastors was sent to the active membership of the congregation, sharing information about the marital separation, the resignation, and the author's hope to remain. The sermon reflects the tension the author experienced between acknowledging her own pain and caring for the congregation in their grief. It also shows how closely related personal and congregational crises can be, and how good preaching can reach in both directions.

Scripture: Ecclesiastes 3:1-8
　　　　　2 Corinthians 4:5-10

The author of Ecclesiastes spoke from personal experience in writing:

> For everything there is a season, and a time for every matter under heaven:
>
> a time to be born, and a time to die;
> a time to plant, and a time to pluck up what is planted;
> a time to kill, and a time to heal;
> a time to break down, and a time to build up;
> a time to weep, and a time to laugh;
> a time to mourn, and a time to dance;
> a time to throw away stones, and a time to gather stones together;
> a time to embrace, and a time to refrain from embracing;
> a time to seek, and a time to lose;
> a time to keep, and a time to throw away;
> a time to tear, and a time to sew;
> a time to keep silence, and a time to speak;
> a time to love, and a time to hate;
> a time for war, and a time for peace.

I would add from my, and our, personal experience:

> a time for action, and a time for reflection;
> a time for despair, and a time for hope;
> a time for pain, and a time for healing;
> a time for brokenness, and a time for shalom;
> a time for doubt, and a time for faith;
> a time for weakness, and a time for strength;
> a time for holding on, and a time for letting go;
> a time for emptying, and a time for filling;
> a time to hold one's breath and wait,
> and a time to take a deep breath and plunge in!

To everything there is a season. *I* have entered a new season in *my* life, and *we* have passed into a new season together. It is a passage I would just as soon not make. It is a passage from which I would have wished to protect you. But that is not the way it is for us today.

So I will begin by sharing a painful moment with you from very early in my ministry. It occurred the first Sunday in May of 1977. I was serving as pastor for a small rural congregation. It was Country Church Day, the biggest day of the year for that congregation. This is a day set aside to celebrate and lift up the values inherent in rural life and simple living.

The sanctuary is always crowded for morning worship on Country Church Day. After the service the congregation pours out the doors to enjoy "dinner on the grounds." Then in the afternoon the sanctuary is jammed again to hear the special speaker of the day—usually a high-ranking state government official—deliver a message on the kinds of values that are represented in rural life.

The first Sunday in May 1977 was my initial experience with Country Church Day. I was extremely nervous and anxious about every detail. After all, I was still a seminarian, halfway between the pulpit and the pew. Unsure of myself. Inexperienced. It turned out to be a wonderful, exhilarating day.

The one memory that stands out in my mind was eating lunch with John and Susan [not their real names], long-time members of the congregation. He was a deacon. We stood under the trees and leaned against the hood of their car. We talked about the weather and the delicious food and anticipated the afternoon speaker. Nothing out of the ordinary passed between us. I thought how good it was to have a deacon like John in the church.

Three days later, on Wednesday afternoon, while Susan was working at the bank, John wrote her a note and left it on the kitchen table. Then he took his gun, climbed the hill to the barn, went inside, turned the gun on himself and committed suicide.

The bullet shattered more than his body. It jolted a whole community; it tore at the fabric of a congregation and it made me aware of how one act, even one word, when enacted or spoken, can forever and irrevocably alter life's circumstances.

The moment I received the call about John I grew up a lot. I did not know it then, but I did later. And I learned some things about myself and about life in the immediacy of that time that are more true now than ever:

- I am fallible. I miss signals. I make mistakes. Perhaps there was no signal from John, but if there was, I missed it.
- I am not a Savior. I cannot save anyone, least of all myself, from the agonies that accompany human existence. I cannot make things all better or take away the pain. I can only *point* to the Savior, to the One who takes the pains and hurts upon Himself.
- I am a sinner. I participate in the brokenness of the human condition. I need the grace and mercy of God as much as anyone.
- No one is immune to anything, no matter their status or vocation in life.
- People carry enormous burdens around with them—burdens that are not visible to the naked eye, but which debilitate and hurt and dissipate energy.

It was sometime during the twenty-minute drive to Susan's after the call came to me that afternoon that I was struck by the gravity of the situation. I was the pastor of the church and somehow or other I was going to have to stand before the family and the congregation and the curiosity seekers in a couple of days at John's funeral to say something of comfort and to try to make sense out of what was essentially senseless. That was the hardest preaching assignment I have ever had—until today.

Of course, I could not "make sense" out of that tragic ending to a life that had had value and purpose. I could only acknowledge for all of us, including myself, that there were no easy answers, and perhaps no answers at all, to the questions that crowded our minds. The only answer lay in God's comforting presence and faithful promise to turn death into life.

I do not find that easy to live with, but I do know it to be true. You see, I was taught in grammar that you never leave participles dangling. I was taught in music theory that you never leave a seventh chord unresolved. If you do, there is incompleteness in the thought and tension in the music.

But I have learned that in life there are dangling participles and unresolved chords all over the place. That life is characterized more by ambiguity than certainty, more by change than permanence, more by tension than resolution. And this week we have come face to face with one of the most troubling ambiguities of all—the unraveling of a relationship that appeared to have substance and permanence to it.

I can get through this terrible time because I know I have a treasure inside of me, the luster of which has not been dulled by the tarnishing and punishing events of this last week, or of the long months that preceded it. That treasure is my sense of call by God. That sense has not wavered in all the struggle that my family and I have been through. I have struggled with other things, such as personal authority issues. I have been fearful of my reception in the community after this. I have dreaded this day especially. I have doubted some of my competencies and wondered about my abilities. But I have never doubted my call from God to preach the gospel, to stand as a representative of Christ in your midst, to minister to you to the best of my ability, and to receive ministry from you.

I can get through because I know that I am not alone. There are people who are standing here with me this morning, who are holding me and you in their thoughts and prayers. I can feel their strength from across town and across the miles.

And ultimately I can get through because I know there is Someone standing with me at this very moment who knows the pain better than I know it myself and who shares the burden of this time in the most profound way. That same Someone, God, is sitting with you right now, too, and is aware of your sadness and anger and bewilderment and disillusionment and embarrassment.

You see, I believe with Paul that this is a transitory affliction, that it has the capacity to make us a stronger community in the long run. Yes, "we are afflicted in every way, but not crushed; perplexed, but not driven to despair; persecuted, but not forsaken; struck down, but not destroyed."

We will continue to strive and to thrive not because of who we are but because of Whose we are. And God has the power to turn even this crucible experience into the dawning of a new day. I believe that. I hope you do, too.

Today is a strange day for all of us. It is awkward and painful. It is also strange for me that this particular day should fall in the calendar on May Day. A day that in its very name suggests the ambiguities of life.

May Day is a time of celebration. A time to rejoice in spring. A time to dance. Mayday is also the international distress signal. I am putting out a distress signal today. I am asking you to support and minister to me and to my family. In fact you are already doing that in a most remarkable and gratifying way.

I do not feel like dancing around a maypole today, but I might be persuaded to do a two-step around the cross. I do not say that to trivialize or show disrespect to the most profound symbol of human suffering that exists. I say it because the cross represents God's answer to the mayday signal I have sent out and that we are sending out together. The cross is a message from God that says, "I will not desert you. I will shoulder the burden with you. I will take the pain upon myself. And together we will continue the journey 'bloodied but unbowed.'"

The words of Paul have stood behind and permeated this sermon today. They have encouraged me and allowed me to add a glimmer of hope to the deep sadness and desolation I feel. Paul was speaking in Second Corinthians of his own struggles in ministry and of the ups and downs that the early church community experienced. His words acknowledged the ambiguity they all faced. But they also acknowledged the hope which lies at the core of the Christian faith. They are words which say what I need to have said to me today and what I want, at heart and at last, on this day to say to you:

> For we do not proclaim ourselves; we proclaim Jesus Christ as Lord, and ourselves as your slaves for Jesus' sake. For it is the God who said, "Let light shine out of darkness," who has shone in our hearts to give the light of the knowledge of the glory of God in the face of Jesus Christ. But we have this treasure in clay jars, so that it may be made clear that this extraordinary power belongs to God and does not come from us. We are afflicted in every way, but not crushed; perplexed, but not driven to despair; persecuted, but not forsaken; struck down, but not destroyed; always carrying in the body the death of Jesus, so that the life of Jesus may also be made visible in our bodies.

Amen.

NOTES

INTRODUCTION

1. I first heard this story from Ann and Randy Updegraff Spleth. It was confirmed for me by Boutellier.
2. Howard W. Stone, *Crisis Counseling*, revised edition (Minneapolis: Augsburg Fortress, 1993), 9.
3. James S. Oglesby, lecture given at Brite Divinity School, Fort Worth, Tex., 1 July 1993.

I. TYPES OF CRISES

1. R. L. Pavelsky, "Crisis Intervention Theory," *Dictionary of Pastoral Care and Counseling,* ed. Rodney J. Hunter (Nashville: Abingdon, 1990), 245. David Switzer writes: "*Homeostasis* refers simply to a relative balance of internal forces with one another, and can be extended even to mean a relative balance between internal and external demands." David K. Switzer, *The Minister as Crisis Counselor,* revised edition (Nashville: Abingdon, 1986), 37.
2. William Butler Yeats, "The Second Coming," *The Collected Poems of W. B. Yeats* (New York: Macmillan, 1956), 184.
3. Charles Gerkin, cited in Stone, *Crisis Counseling,* revised edition (Minneapolis: Augsburg Fortress, 1993), 12.
4. Harry Emerson Fosdick, "When Life Reaches Its Depths," *Riverside Sermons* (New York: Harper and Bros., 1958), 47.
5. Charles J. Stewart and Bruce Kendall, eds., *A Man Named John F. Kennedy: Sermons on His Assassination* (Glen Rock, N.J.: Paulist, 1964); Ignacio Castuera, ed., *Dreams on Fire, Embers of Hope: From the Pulpits of Los Angeles After the Riots* (St. Louis: Chalice, 1992); and Marsha Bishop, ed., *And the Angels Wept* (St. Louis: Chalice, 1995).
6. Arthur John Gossip, "But When Life Tumbles In, What Then?" *The Hero in Thy Soul* (Edinburgh: T. & T. Clark, 1928), 106-16.
7. David Buttrick, *Homiletic* (Philadelphia: Fortress, 1987), 405.

II. PSYCHOLOGY OF THE CRISIS EXPERIENCE

1. Charles Kemp, Edgar Jackson, and Donald Capps have produced what little work has been done, along with Howard Stone's interesting *The Word of God and Pastoral Care* (Nashville: Abingdon, 1988).
2. Howard Clinebell, *Basic Types of Pastoral Care and Counseling*, revised edition (Nashville: Abingdon, 1984), 40.
3. William Willimon, *Integrative Preaching* (Nashville: Abingdon, 1981), 37-38.
4. See Stone, *The Word of God and Pastoral Care*, 27-31.
5. Stone, *Crisis Counseling*, revised edition (Minneapolis: Augsburg Fortress, 1993), 13. This understanding may be traced to Gerald Caplan, *Principles of Preventive Psychiatry* (New York: Basic Books, 1964).
6. For a discussion of these developmental crises, see Erik H. Erikson, *Childhood and Society*, revised (New York: Norton, 1963).
7. Stone, *Crisis Counseling*, 13.
8. Andrew Lester, lecture at Brite Divinity School, Fort Worth, Tex., 24 June 1993.
9. Carl S. Dudley and Melvin E. Schoonover, "After the Hurricane," *The Christian Century* (2-9 June 1993): 588.
10. See Andrew D. Lester, *Hope in Pastoral Care and Counseling* (Louisville: Westminster/John Knox, 1995).
11. See Switzer's diagram on the development of situational crises in *The Minister as Crisis Counselor*, revised edition (Nashville: Abingdon, 1986), 45.

III. THEOLOGY AND CRISIS

1. See Ronald Allen, "New Directions for Homiletics," *Journal for Preachers* 16 (Easter 1993): 20-26, and Charles L. Campbell, *Preaching Jesus* (Grand Rapids, Mich.: Eerdmans, 1997), xi-xiii.
2. Paul Scott Wilson, *The Practice of Preaching* (Nashville: Abingdon, 1995), 68. See also Stone, *The Word of God and Pastoral Care* (Nashville: Abingdon, 1988), chapter 4.
3. Wilson, *The Practice of Preaching*, 70.
4. Susan J. White, *Christian Worship and Technological Change* (Nashville: Abingdon, 1994), 114-15.
5. I first heard this phrase from my dear friend and teacher K. Morgan Edwards in the late 1970s. I do not know if it was original with him.
6. I find it significant that serious crises embed themselves in our memories in ways that other events do not. Most older Americans can tell you exactly where they were and what they were doing when the news of the attack on Pearl Harbor came to them on Sunday, December 7, 1941. I can still give an almost minute-by-minute account of my experiences on Friday, November 22, 1963, the day John F. Kennedy was assassinated.
7. I have this story from Gilbert Davis.
8. Ronald J. Allen, *Preaching the Topical Sermon* (Louisville: Westminster/John Knox, 1992), 21-22. Although we will look at understanding and decision separately, they are, of course, inextricably intertwined.
9. I have adapted this list of concerns from the aforementioned lecture by Andrew Lester.

10. William Sloan Coffin, "Sermon for Alex," reprinted in *The Lutheran Standard* (20 April 1984): 5.
11. My one theatrical experience was as part of the cast for a performance of Guenter Rutenborn's splendid play *The Sign of Jonah*. After a trial God is pronounced guilty for our sorry situation and sentenced to become one of us. People leave the theater realizing that the sentence has already been carried out.
12. See Rodney R. Hutton, "Slogans in the Midst of Crisis: Jeremiah and His Adversaries," *Word and World* 10:3 (Summer 1990): 230.
13. Howard Clinebell, *Basic Types of Pastoral Care and Counseling*, revised edition (Nashville: Abingdon, 1984), 50.
14. Stone, *The Word of God and Pastoral Care*, 162.
15. Ibid., 162. Stone suggests a method for doing this.
16. See Joseph R. Jeter Jr., *Re/Membering: Meditations and Sermons for the Table of Jesus Christ* (St. Louis: Chalice Press, 1995), 147-148.
17. Urban T. Holmes, "Worship and Aging: Memory and Repentence," in *Ministry with the Aging*, ed. William M. Clements (San Francisco: Harper & Row, 1981), 92.
18. Dietrich Ritschl, *Memory and Hope* (New York: Macmillan, 1967), 218.
19. Arthur John Gossip, "But When Life Tumbles In, What Then?" *The Hero in Thy Soul* (Edinburgh: T. & T. Clark, 1928), 111.
20. I first heard this tradition from Ronald E. Osborn. See the slightly different version in Jeter, *Re/Membering*, 46-49.
21. Alexander Campbell, cited in Joseph R. Jeter Jr. and Hiram J. Lester, "The Tragedy of Wickliffe Campbell," *Lexington Theological Quarterly* 22:3 (July 1987), 93.
22. Martin E. Marty, "God's Will," *The Christian Century* (26 October 1983): 975.
23. Elie Wiesel, *Night* (New York: Bantam, 1960), 62.
24. When I preached this sermon thirteen years ago, that was a completely ridiculous assertion. Now I am not so sure. Yesterday's hyperbole becomes today's reality. Any analogy about things "amazing" or "ridiculous" quickly becomes dated.
25. From "If You Will Go With Us ...," preached at the General Assembly of the Christian Church (Disciples of Christ) in the United States and Canada, Des Moines, Iowa, 7 August 1985.
26. Samuel Terrien, *The Elusive Presence* (San Francisco: Harper and Row, 1978), 26-27.
27. Ibid., 476.
28. Ibid., 470.
29. See Eugene Boring, "Everything Is Going to Be All Right," *Preaching Through the Apocalypse*, ed. Cornish R. Rogers and Joseph R. Jeter Jr., (St. Louis: Chalice, 1992), 75-82.
30. James A. Wharton, sermon at TCU Ministers Week, Fort Worth, Tex., 4 Feb, 1985.
31. Alfred Tennyson, "In Memoriam," stanza liv, *Poetical Works* (London: Oxford University Press, 1953), 243.
32. Edward Schillebeeckx, cited in Geoffrey Wainwright, "Preaching as Worship," *Theories of Preaching*, ed. Richard Lischer (Durham, N.C.: Labyrinth Press, 1987), 362.
33. Boring, "Everything Is Going to Be All Right," 82.
34. Buttrick, quoted in Allen, *Preaching the Topical Sermon*, 22.
35. I am indebted to Rebekah Miles for the pilgrimage language used in this section.
36. A Hausa phrase I heard frequently while living in the Republic of the Niger.
37. Lewis Carroll, *Alice in Wonderland*, vol. 5 (New York: Collier, 1938), 51.

38. This exercise originated with Native Americans, was refined by Sister José Hobday, and written down by Sister Dorothy Powers, unpublished manuscript, no date.
39. These "directional vignettes" are adapted from presentations I made at the Brite Summer Institute, Santa Fe, N.Mex., 13-17 July 1992.
40. Adapted from a speech I made to the Disciples Ministerial Association of the Pacific Southwest Region of the Christian Church (Disciples of Christ) at Claremont, Calif., 13 Nov 1984, and published as "Kadesh-Barnea, CA" in *Impact* (Claremont) 13 (1984), 17-21.
41. The following section is adapted from a sermon I preached before a conference on "Preaching, Worship and the Lukan Passion" at Santa Barbara, Calif., 11 February 1992.
42. Harry Chapin, "Goin' to Atlanta," *Cotton Patch Gospel*, video produced by Philip M. Getter, directed by Russell Treyz. Copyright 1982 Sandy Songs.
43. Carmen Bernos de Gasztold, *Prayers from the Ark*, trans. Rumer Godden (New York: The Viking Press, 1962), 61.
44. Zora Neale Hurston, *Their Eyes Were Watching God* (Urbana: University of Illinois Press, 1978), 136-37. See Jeter, *Re/Membering . . .*, 122-23.
45. Robert A. Caro, *The Years of Lyndon Johnson: The Path to Power* (New York: Vintage Books, 1983), 247.
46. See Joseph A. Fitzmyer, *The Gospel According to Luke, I-IX* (Garden City, N.Y.: Doubleday, 1981), 828.
47. See, for example, Craig A. Evans, "He Set His Face," *Biblica* 63 (April 1982): 545-48, and "He Set His Face . . . Once Again," *Biblica* 68 (January 1987): 80-84.
48. See Fred Craddock, *Luke* (Louisville: John Knox, 1990), 142.
49. John Deschner, sermon preached at TCU Ministers Week, Fort Worth, Tex., 10 February 1987.
50. Martin Pike, cited in a sermon by Bryan Feille, South Hills Christian Church, Fort Worth, Tex., Advent 1990.
51. James Fenhagen, *More than Wanderers* (New York: Seabury, 1978), paraphrased in a sermon by Bryan Feille at South Hills Christian Church, Fort Worth, Tex., Lent 1985
52. J. R. R. Tolkien, *The Hobbit* (Boston: Houghton Mifflin, 1966), cited by Feille.
53. John Muir, *Son of the Wilderness*, ed. Linnie Marsh Wolfe (Madison: University of Wisconsin, 1978), 169.
54. François Fénelon, *Selections from the Writings of François Fénelon* (Nashville: Upper Room, 1962), 17.
55. Thomas R. Kelly, *Selections from A Testament of Devotion*, ed. Douglas V. Steere (Nashville: Upper Room, 1955), 7.
56. 2 Samuel 5:22-25 gives good witness to this. God tells David to put his enemies (the Philistines) between himself and his security (Jerusalem). It took considerable faith to do that, as it did for Abraham on Mount Moriah in Genesis 22.
57. John Bunyan, *Pilgrim's Progress* (London: Oxford University Press, 1902), 130.
58. Excerpted from Parker J. Palmer, "Escape and Engagement," *Pendle Hill Bulletin* 270 (March 1975), 7.
59. Eugene Lowry, sermon preached at the annual meeting of the Academy of Homiletics, Pasadena, Calif., 6 December 1991, cited in Jeter, *Re/Membering*, 90.
60. See Thomas Troeger's marvelous sermon on this text from Matthew 2 in *Imagining a Sermon* (Nashville: Abingdon, 1990), 61-65.
61. Martha J. Simmons, "On the Making of a Homiletician," in *Preaching on the Brink*, ed. Martha J. Simmons (Nashville: Abingdon, 1996), 19.
62. Contrast this with the parable of the unjust steward in Luke 16. Some inter-

preters throw up their hands at this difficult parable and say, "What it must mean is that sometime you've just got to do something." Sometimes, perhaps. Other times, no.

63. He denied it was an autobiography, which is why I do not use that term.

64. Nikos Kazantzakis, *Report to Greco,* trans. P. A. Bien (New York: Simon and Schuster, 1965), 511-12.

65. Albert M. Pennybacker, "What to Do When You Don't Know What to Do Next," *The Vital Pulpit of the Christian Church,* ed. Hunter Beckelhymer (St. Louis: Bethany, 1969), 278-79. Used with permission.

IV. WORSHIP AND PREACHING IN CRISIS

1. David Nelson Duke and Paul D. Duke, *Anguish and the Word: Preaching That Touches Pain* (Greenville, S.C.: Smyth & Helwys, 1992), 21.

2. Kazantzakis, *Report to Greco,* trans. P. A. Bien (New York: Simon and Schuster, 1965), 88.

3. See Duke and Duke, 21-25.

4. C. Ellis Nelson, "The Habitat of the Spirit," *Princeton Seminary Bulletin* 1:3 (New Series, 1977): 111.

5. Elisha A. Hoffman, "Leaning on the Everlasting Arms," 1887.

6. William Willimon, *Worship as Pastoral Care* (Nashville: Abingdon, 1979), 100.

7. Edward Norbeck, cited in William Willimon, *The Service of God* (Nashville: Abingdon, 1983), 43.

8. Fosdick, "What Is the Matter with Preaching?" *Harper's Magazine* 157 (July 1928): 135.

9. Adapted from David James Randolph, "Carl Michaelson's Theology of Preaching," in *Hermeneutics and the Worldliness of Faith,* ed. Charles Courtney et al., published as a special edition of *The Drew Gateway* 45, no. 1-3 (1974–75): 74.

10. Edward Shils, "Ritual and Crisis," in *The Religious Situation: 1968,* ed. Donald R. Cutler (Boston: Beacon, 1968), 736.

11. Craddock, lecture given at Methodist Preaching Conference, Lake Arrowhead, Calif., spring 1981.

12. Colbert S. Cartwright, *Candles of Grace* (St. Louis: Chalice, 1992), 17-18.

13. A remembered line from an early 1980s lecture by Ronald E. Osborn, School of Theology at Claremont, Claremont, Calif.

14. Thomas G. Long, *The Witness of Preaching* (Louisville: Westminster John Knox, 1989), 47.

15. Jurgen Moltmann says, "The proclamation of the gospel always belongs within a community, for every language lives in a community or creates one." Cited in Long, 47.

16. Bruce Birch, cited in Denise Dombkowski Hopkins, "Failing Brain, Faithful Community," *Memphis Theological Seminary Journal* 32, no. 3 (fall 1994): 36.

17. See Don E. Saliers, *Worship as Theology* (Nashville: Abingdon, 1994), 86.

18. Arthur John Gossip, "But When Life Tumbles In, What Then?" *The Hero in Thy Soul* (Edinburgh: T. & T. Clark, 1928), 234.

19. Carol Doran and Thomas H. Troeger, *Open to Glory* (Valley Forge, Penn.: Judson, 1983), 80.

20. See Saliers, chapters 5-8.

21. I have this from Charles Kemp.

22. John Knox, *The Integrity of Preaching* (Nashville: Abingdon, 1957), 76, quoted in

Willimon, *Integrative Preaching* (Nashville: Abingdon, 1981), 90.
23. Geoffrey Wainwright, "Preaching as Worship," in *Theories of Preaching*, ed. Richard Lischer (Durham, N.C.: Labyrinth, 1987), 353.
24. Wainwright, 358-363.
25. David Buttrick, *A Captive Voice* (Louisville: Westminster John Knox, 1994), 45.

V. CRISIS PREACHING: SOME HOMILETICAL STRATEGIES

1. Sandra Lydick, "Is New Age and Humanistic Philosophy a Peril?" in *Aledo United Methodist Church Newsletter*, Aledo, Tex., 10 February 1993.
2. Gene Garrison, "Confronting Crises with Grace and Truth," in *Preach the Word in Love and Power*, ed. James C. Barry (Nashville: Convention Press, 1986), 72.
3. See Abraham Heschel, *The Prophets* (New York: Harper, 1962), chapter 1, for a good discussion of the prophetic function.
4. John Milton, *Paradise Lost*, book viii, line 352 (Cambridge: University Press, 1934), 225-26.
5. Bryan Feille first pointed this out to me. For more on the Rumpelstiltskin effect, see E. Fuller Torrey, *Witchdoctors and Psychiatrists* (New York: Jason Aronson, 1983).
6. Jim W. Corder, lecture given at Texas Christian University, 25 November 1963.
7. The eulogy was published in *Unity* (May-June 1984). It may also be found in Amiri Baraka, *Eulogies* (New York: Marsilio, 1996), 48-54.
8. See Delbert R. Hillers, *Lamentations* (Garden City, N.Y.: Doubleday, 1972), xl-xli. See also Norman Gottwald, *Studies in the Book of Lamentations* (Chicago: A. R. Allenson, 1954), especially chapter 6, for interesting material on the significance and use of Lamentations. Emilie Townes, in a lecture at Brite Divinity School, Fort Worth, Tex., 4 October 1995, suggested that, biblically speaking, lamentation often moves into apocalypse, which moves into hope.
9. Walt Whitman, "When Lilacs Last in the Dooryard Bloom'd," *Leaves of Grass*, ed. Emory Holloway (Garden City: Doubleday, 1957), 275.
10. Ellen Zetzel Lambert, *Placing Sorrow* (Chapel Hill: University of North Carolina Press, 1976), xiii, xv.
11. John Wesley, "The Sunday Service," in *Liturgies of the Western Church*, ed. Bard Thompson (Philadelphia: Fortress, 1961), 416.
12. *The Book of Common Prayer* (1979), 320-21.
13. Ibid., 323.
14. Walter Brueggemann, "Is There No Balm in Gilead?" *Sojourners* (October 1985), 29.
15. Sanders' sermon was published in his book *God Has a Story, Too* (Philadelphia: Fortress, 1979).
16. Chrysostom's "Homilies on the Statues" are published in *The Nicene and Post-Nicene Fathers*, First Series, ed. Philip Schaff (Grand Rapids: Eerdmans, 1956), vol. IX, 317-489. For this quotation, see 344-45.
17. See David Gregg, "The Sacramental Wagons," in *Modern Sermons by World Scholars*, ed. Robert Scott & William C. Stiles (New York: Funk & Wagnalls, 1909), vol. IV, 101-20. These old anthologies are gold mines of homiletical insight and material.
18. Martin Luther, "The Sixth Sermon, March 14, 1522, Friday after Invocavit" in

Luther's Works, vol. 51, ed. & trans. John W. Doberstein (Philadelphia: Fortress, 1959), 95, cited in Joseph R. Jeter Jr., *Re/Membering: Meditations and Sermons for the Table of Jesus Christ* (St. Louis: Chalice Press, 1995), 70.

19. Jeter, *Re/Membering,* 70.

20. Leonard Sweet, "Not All Cats Are Gray: Beyond Liberalism's Uncertain Faith," *The Christian Century,* (23-30 June 1982): 721-25.

21. Ronald Osborn, "Brand," *Impact* (Claremont), no. 2 (1979): 37.

22. St. Ambrose, cited in Geoffrey Wainwright, *Eucharist and Eschatology* (New York: Oxford University Press, 1981), 153.

23. The Wittenburg Sermons of 1522 are published in *Luther's Works,* vol. 51, 67-100. This quotation is from pp. 99-100.

24. Alex Haley, *Roots,* television miniseries, 1977.

25. I am aware that the five suggestions I have made may be seen as inconsistent with one another. But I stand by the suggestions, which are different because crises are different. Certain situations will call for certain responses.

26. Again, I first heard this story in a lecture years ago by Ronald Osborn, who has taught me so much. More recently, I heard the story repeated by Jorge Lara-Braud in a lecture at Brite Divinity School, Fort Worth, Texas, 21 October 1992, marking the quincentennial of Columbus' "discovery" of America. The original source is Bartolomé de Las Casas, *Historia de Las Indias,* ed. Agustin Millares Carlo (Mexico, D.F.: Fondo de Cultura Economica, 1951), vol. 2, 441-42.

VI. THE STRUCTURE OF THE CRISIS SERMON

1. Paul Scott Wilson, *The Practice of Preaching* (Nashville: Abingdon, 1995), 215.

2. Ibid., 200.

3. Howard W. Stone, *Crisis Counseling,* revised edition (Minneapolis: Augsburg Fortress, 1993), 38.

4. I am relying on memory for this story. I have searched for it in print, but without success.

5. James A. Michener, *Centennial* (New York: Random House, 1974), 615.

6. Ibid., 616.

7. Fred B. Craddock, *Preaching* (Nashville: Abingdon, 1985), 123.

8. Craddock, lecture given at Methodist Preaching Conference, Lake Arrowhead, Calif., 1981.

9. Stone, *Crisis Counseling,* 27-28.

10. Ibid., 28.

11. Fred B. Craddock, *As One Without Authority* (Nashville: Abingdon, 1979), 57. I have adapted the illustration, so that the logical beginning of each method rests on the bottom.

12. I am aware that the language of deduction and induction has been stretched almost beyond viability in preaching and that it is not the language of the moment. I use it because it was used when these examples were given.

13. Katie Sherrod, lecture at Brite Divinity School, Fort Worth, Tex., 25 June 1993.

14. Ronald J. Allen, *Preaching the Topical Sermon* (Louisville: Westminster/John Knox, 1992), 16.

15. See *Life, Letters, Lectures and Addresses of Frederick W. Robertson,* ed. Stopford Brooke (New York: Harper and Bros., 1870), 315. See also my article on Robert-

son in *The Concise Encyclopedia of Preaching*, ed. William H. Willimon and Richard Lischer (Louisville: Westminster/John Knox, 1995), 418-20.

16. The *mogen David*, with its emphasis on "the protection of God," was in the ancient world not limited to use by Jews. It is found in some medieval cathedrals as well as synagogues.

17. See Craddock's "particulars of experience" in *As One Without Authority*, 57; Eugene Lowry's "upsetting the equilibrium" in *The Homiletical Plot* (Atlanta: John Knox, 1980), 28-35; and Wilson's "judgment" in *The Practice of Preaching*, 148ff.

18. See Craddock's "general truth," 57; Lowry's "experiencing the gospel," 62-66; and Wilson's "grace," 148ff.

19. DeWayne Renfro, "And on the Third Day," sermon preached at Brite Divinity School, Fort Worth, Tex., November 1994. Used with permission.

VII. BIBLICAL RESOURCES FOR CRISIS SERMONS: AN ANNOTATED LECTIONARY

1. Emilie Townes, lecture given at Brite Divinity School, Fort Worth, Tex., 4 October 1995.

2. See Consultation on Common Texts, *The Revised Common Lectionary* (Nashville: Abingdon, 1992), 11.

3. Thomas G. Long, *Preaching and the Literary Forms of the Bible* (Philadelphia: Fortress, 1989), 47.

4. Tanya Tucker "Two Sparrows in a Hurricane" (Liberty 56825, 1992).

5. Sören Kierkegaard, *The Gospel of Our Sufferings*, trans. A. S. Aldworth and W. S. Ferrie (Grand Rapids, Mich.: Eerdmans, 1964), 114.

6. Thomas G. Long is preparing a new study of the funeral and the funeral sermon.

7. Richard P. Lord and Janice Harris Lord, "Out of the Depths: Helps for Clergy in Ministering to Crime Victims," unpublished manuscript, 1993.

8. Dylan Thomas, "And Death Shall Have No Dominion," *The Collected Poems of Dylan Thomas* (New York: New Directions, 1953), 77.

9. See chapter 3 in William Stringfellow, *An Ethic for Christian and Other Aliens in a Strange Land* (Waco, Tex.: Word, 1973).

10. Walter Harrelson, cited in Toni Craven, *The Book of Psalms* (Collegeville, Minn.: Liturgical Press, 1992), 50.

11. Phyllis Trible, *Texts of Terror* (Philadelphia: Fortress, 1984), 37-65.

12. Nikos Kazantzakis, *Report to Greco* (New York: Simon and Schuster, 1965), 59-60.

13. See Richard P. Lord's important essay "Do I Have to Forgive?" *The Christian Century* (9 October 1981): 902-3.

14. Fred B. Craddock, lecture given at the First Christian Church of Whittier, Calif., 1981.

15. Daniel T. Hans, "Preaching Through Personal Pain," *Leadership* (winter 1989): 35-39.

16. Harry Emerson Fosdick, "The Great Hours of a Man's Life," *Riverside Sermons* (New York: Harper and Bros., 1958), 16.

17. John Bunyan, *Pilgrim's Progress*, paraphrased by Arthur John Gossip, "But When Life Tumbles In, What Then?" *The Hero in Thy Soul* (Edinburgh: T. & T. Clark, 1928), 116.

18. Charlie W. Shedd, *Remember, I Love You: Martha's Story* (Carmel, N.Y.: Guide-posts, 1990), 164-67.
19. William Maxwell, *Ancestors* (New York: Alfred A. Knoph, 1971), 290.
20. Ibid.
21. Douglas R. Miller, "Train Won't Run on a Torn-up Track," sermon preached at Brite Divinity School, Fort Worth, Tex., 8 July 1993.
22. Steve Clark and Johnny MacRae, "When You Leave That Way, You Can Never Go Back" (Atlantic 87357, 1992), performed by the group Confederate Railroad and cited in Miller's sermon.
23. Gary Parker, *The Gift of Doubt* (San Francisco: Harper & Row, 1990), cited in Miller's sermon.
24. Sheldon Kopp, *If You Meet the Buddha on the Road, Kill Him* (Ben Lomond, Calif.: Science and Behavior Books, 1972), 158.
25. Ibid.
26. See the marvelous sermon on this text by David and Paul Duke, "The Tree, the Cave and Beyond," in *Anguish and the Word*, 63-68.

VIII. CRISIS SERMONS

1. Colbert Cartwright died April 13, 1996. Our last conversation was about this sermon. The language of 1957 has been retained.
2. Jodi Enda, "Little Rock Nine Return as Heroes," *Fort Worth Star-Telegram* (26 September 1997): A-1.
3. See Kevin Sack, "Central High School to Mark Integration History," *Fort Worth Star-Telegram* (21 September 1997): A-18. See also Paul Greenberg, "Editorial," *Fort Worth Star-Telegram* (26 September 1997): B-9, who interviewed Eckford, as Cartwright had forty years earlier: "Of the Little Rock Nine who were refused admission to Central that fateful day, Elizabeth Eckford may be the one you remember from the photographs. She's the graceful black teenager in a white dress walking slowly through the gauntlet, the picture of grace under pressure. Here is her memory of one indelible moment: 'I tried to see a friendly face somewhere in the mob—someone who maybe would help. I looked into the face of an old woman, and it seemed a kind face, but when I looked at her again, she spat on me.' "
4. Jo Pendleton is the author of this prayer. It is used with her permission.
5. Annette Sowell is the pastor of the church where this sermon was delivered. Sermon used with permission.
6. William H. Willimon, "When Bad Things Happen to Good People," *Pulpit Resource* 23:1 (January-March 1995): 49.
7. G. Reneé Ahern, "For the Little Ones," *Biblical Preaching Journal* 7 (summer 1994): 39.
8. Adapted from Robert W. Stackel, "When Life Becomes a Death Valley," *The Clergy Journal* 64 (February 1993): 22.
9. Andraé Crouch, "Through It All," Manna Music, 1971.
10. The sermon was preached without notes. It has been transcribed from a tape recording and, with the preacher's permission, edited by the author for ease of reading. The oral nature of the sermon remains.
11. Proverb from an old wooden plaque found many years ago. Original source is unknown.
12. Gina Rhea remains the pastor of the First Christian Church in Radford, Virginia. Sermon used with permission.

Selected Bibliography

Crisis Preaching: Theory

Allen, Ronald J. *Preaching the Topical Sermon.* Louisville: Westminster/John Knox, 1992.

Buttrick, David. "Preaching and Praxis." In *Homiletic.* Philadelphia: Fortress, 1987.

Capps, Donald. *Pastoral Counseling and Preaching.* Philadelphia: Westminster, 1980.

Jackson, Edgar N. *How to Preach to People's Needs.* New York: Abingdon, 1956.

Kemp, Charles. *Life-Situation Preaching.* St. Louis: Bethany, 1956

Richmond, Kent D. *Preaching to Sufferers.* Nashville: Abingdon, 1988.

Smith, Kelly Miller. *Social Crisis Preaching.* Macon, Ga.: Mercer, 1984.

Willimon, William. *Integrative Preaching.* Nashville: Abingdon, 1981.

Wilson, Paul Scott. *The Practice of Preaching.* Nashville: Abingdon, 1995.

Crisis Counseling

Gerkin, Charles V. *Crisis Experience in Modern Life.* Nashville: Abingdon, 1979.

Stone, Howard W. *Crisis Counseling,* revised edition. Minneapolis: Augsburg Fortress, 1993.

Switzer, David K. *The Minister as Crisis Counselor,* revised edition. Nashville: Abingdon, 1986.

Preaching, Theology, and Worship

Stone, Howard. *The Word of God and Pastoral Care.* Nashville: Abingdon, 1988.

Terrien, Samuel. *The Elusive Presence.* San Francisco: Harper & Row, 1978.
Willimon, William. *Worship as Pastoral Care.* Nashville: Abingdon, 1979.

Public Crises

Bishop, Marsha, ed. *And the Angels Wept.* St. Louis: Chalice Press, 1995. Sermons after the 1995 bombing in Oklahoma City.
Castuera, Ignacio, ed. *Dreams on Fire, Embers of Hope: from the Pulpits of Los Angeles After the Riots.* St. Louis: Chalice, 1992.
Stewart, Charles J. and Bruce Kendall, eds. *A Man Named John F. Kennedy: Sermons on His Assassination.* Glen Rock, N.J.: Paulist, 1964.
For those who face the challenge of preaching during or about war, I recommend five classic books by those who have dealt with the question of war in past generations, preaching both for and against America's participation in war:
Ainslie, Peter. *Christ or Napoleon—Which?* New York: Fleming H. Revell, 1915.
Bainton, Roland. *Christian Attitudes Toward War and Peace.* New York: Abingdon, 1960.
Fosdick, Harry Emerson. "The Unknown Soldier." In *Riverside Sermons.* New York: Harper Bros., 1958.
Poling, Daniel. *A Preacher Looks at War.* New York: Macmillan, 1944.
Weatherhead, Leslie. *Thinking Aloud in War-Time.* New York: Abingdon, 1940.

Congregational Crises

Haugk, Kenneth C. *Antagonists in the Church: How to Identify and Deal with Destructive Conflict.* Minneapolis: Augsburg, 1988.
Hicks, H, Beecher, Jr. *Preaching Through a Storm.* Grand Rapids, Mich.: Zondervan, 1987.
Knights, Ward A., Jr., ed. *Sermons from Hell.* St. Louis: Bethany, 1975.
Willimon, William. *Preaching About Conflict in the Local Church.* Philadelphia: Westminster, 1987.

Personal Crises

Duke, David Nelson and Paul D. Duke. *Anguish and the Word: Preaching that Touches Pain.* Greenville, S.C.: Smyth & Helwys, 1992.

Gossip, Arthur John. "But When Life Tumbles In, What Then?" In *The Hero in Thy Soul*. Edinburgh: T. & T. Clark, 1928.

Milhaven, Annie Lally, ed. *Sermons Seldom Heard: Women Proclaim Their Lives*. New York: Crossroad, 1991.